Zoom Whiteboard

Made Simple

Unlock Your Creativity

Kiet Huynh

Table of Contents

CHAPTER I
Introduction to Zoom Whiteboard

1.1 What is Zoom Whiteboard?

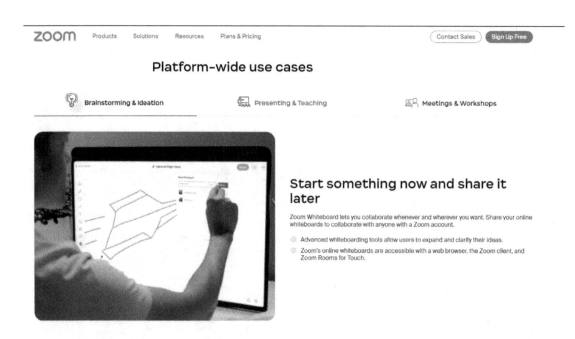

In today's digital world, remote collaboration has become essential for businesses, educators, and teams worldwide. Zoom Whiteboard is a powerful feature integrated into **Zoom Workplace** that allows users to visually collaborate, brainstorm ideas, and organize thoughts in a dynamic and interactive workspace. Unlike traditional whiteboards, which are limited to physical spaces, Zoom Whiteboard enables users to collaborate in real-time from anywhere, making it an indispensable tool for modern teams.

Understanding the Purpose of Zoom Whiteboard

Zoom Whiteboard serves as a **virtual canvas** where individuals and teams can:

A. Sketch out ideas and concepts

B. Create flowcharts and diagrams

C. Brainstorm solutions collaboratively

D. Plan projects and workflows

E. Conduct interactive training and learning sessions

Unlike a simple drawing tool, Zoom Whiteboard is deeply integrated into the Zoom ecosystem, allowing seamless interaction between meetings, chat, and other collaboration tools.

Key Characteristics of Zoom Whiteboard

To better understand Zoom Whiteboard, let's break down its key characteristics:

1. Cloud-Based and Accessible Anywhere

Zoom Whiteboard is entirely cloud-based, meaning that users can access their whiteboards from any device with an internet connection. Whether you are working from your desktop, tablet, or mobile phone, you can create, edit, and share whiteboards in real time.

2. Persistent and Always Available

Unlike a physical whiteboard that gets erased after a meeting, Zoom Whiteboard allows you to save, revisit, and modify your work anytime. It provides a persistent workspace, meaning that you can continue working on a whiteboard over multiple sessions.

3. Real-Time Collaboration with Multiple Users

One of the biggest advantages of Zoom Whiteboard is its ability to support real-time, multi-user collaboration. Team members can work on the same whiteboard simultaneously, adding text, shapes, images, and annotations. Changes are instantly visible to everyone, ensuring seamless teamwork.

4. Deep Integration with Zoom Meetings

Zoom Whiteboard is designed to work hand-in-hand with Zoom Meetings. Users can open a whiteboard during a Zoom call, making it easy to share ideas and engage participants.

Whether you're in a brainstorming session or a project planning meeting, the ability to visualize concepts in real time makes discussions more effective.

5. Easy-to-Use Interface with Intuitive Tools

The Zoom Whiteboard interface is designed to be user-friendly and intuitive. It includes a variety of tools such as:

A.   Drawing tools (pens, highlighters, and erasers)

B.   Shapes and text boxes for structured content

C.   Sticky notes for quick ideas

D.   Images and PDFs to enhance collaboration

E.   Smart connectors for flowcharts and diagrams

Even users with no prior experience in digital whiteboarding can quickly get started and make use of these tools effectively.

How Zoom Whiteboard Compares to Other Digital Whiteboards

While there are several digital whiteboarding tools available, Zoom Whiteboard stands out due to its seamless integration with Zoom Workplace and ease of use. Below is a comparison with some popular alternatives:

Feature	Zoom Whiteboard	Microsoft Whiteboard	Miro	MURAL	Google Jamboard
Integrated with Zoom Meetings	✓ Yes	✗ No	✗ No	✗ No	✗ No
Real-Time Collaboration	✓ Yes	✓ Yes	✓ Yes	✓ Yes	✓ Yes
Cloud-Based & Persistent	✓ Yes	✓ Yes	✓ Yes	✓ Yes	✗ No
Pre-Built Templates	✓ Yes	✓ Yes	✓ Yes	✓ Yes	✗ No
Smart Connectors & Flowcharts	✓ Yes	✗ No	✓ Yes	✓ Yes	✗ No
Offline Access	✗ No	✓ Yes	✗ No	✗ No	✓ Yes

This comparison highlights why Zoom Whiteboard is ideal for users already using Zoom Meetings, making it the go-to choice for integrated collaboration.

Common Use Cases for Zoom Whiteboard

Zoom Whiteboard can be used in various professional and educational scenarios:

1. Business and Team Collaboration

1   Project planning: Teams can use the whiteboard to sketch out project workflows and assign responsibilities.

2   Strategy meetings: Leaders can visualize goals, KPIs, and strategic initiatives.

3   Remote brainstorming: Distributed teams can contribute ideas in real-time, ensuring everyone has a voice.

2. Education and Training

A.   Virtual classrooms: Teachers can create engaging lessons using drawings, annotations, and visuals.

B.   Interactive exercises: Students can participate in group activities using sticky notes and text boxes.

C.   Corporate training: Trainers can illustrate concepts and facilitate workshops in an interactive way.

3. Product and Design Teams

1   UI/UX design: Teams can wireframe apps and websites collaboratively.

2   Concept development: Product managers can map out ideas visually before execution.

3   Workflow visualization: Agile teams can create Kanban boards and sprint plans.

Why Zoom Whiteboard is Essential for Modern Workplaces

With the increasing shift towards remote and hybrid work models, digital collaboration tools like Zoom Whiteboard have become crucial for maintaining productivity. Here's why:

1.   **Breaks communication barriers**: Visual collaboration ensures that teams are on the same page, reducing misunderstandings.

2.   **Enhances engagement**: Interactive features keep participants actively involved in discussions.

3.   **Saves time**: Rather than writing lengthy emails or documents, teams can quickly sketch out ideas and reach decisions faster.

4. **Supports remote work culture**: Employees working from different locations can collaborate just as effectively as those in an office setting.

Conclusion

Zoom Whiteboard is a powerful, versatile, and intuitive tool that enhances teamwork, creativity, and productivity. Whether you're a business professional, educator, designer, or project manager, mastering Zoom Whiteboard will help you collaborate more effectively and bring ideas to life.

In the next chapter, we'll explore how to get started with Zoom Whiteboard, including how to access and set up your first whiteboard session.

1.2 Why Use Zoom Whiteboard?

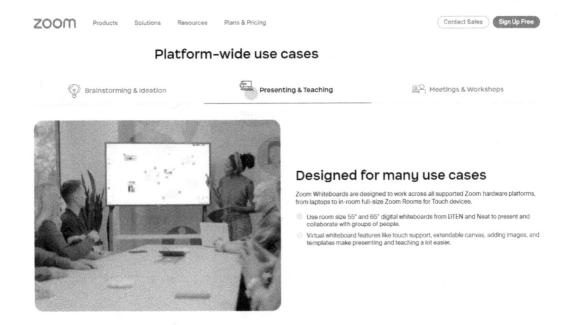

In today's fast-paced digital world, remote collaboration has become an essential part of business, education, and creative work. Zoom Whiteboard offers a powerful solution for teams and individuals looking to brainstorm, plan, and collaborate visually—no matter where they are. But why should you use Zoom Whiteboard over other tools? This section explores the key advantages, real-world applications, and how this feature can enhance your workflow.

Enhancing Collaboration in a Virtual Environment

One of the biggest challenges of remote work is effective collaboration. Traditional video conferencing tools allow for verbal discussions, but they often lack the interactive element needed for brainstorming, planning, and idea sharing. Zoom Whiteboard bridges this gap by providing a shared virtual space where users can visually express their thoughts in real-time.

Real-Time Collaboration Across Locations

With Zoom Whiteboard, team members can work together synchronously or asynchronously, making it a great tool for distributed teams. Whether you're in a live meeting or adding ideas to a shared board before a scheduled discussion, Zoom Whiteboard ensures continuous collaboration.

Engagement and Interaction

Instead of relying on passive communication (e.g., long emails or static slide decks), Zoom Whiteboard engages users actively. Team members can draw, annotate, and move elements freely, making discussions more dynamic and productive.

A Versatile Tool for Different Use Cases

Zoom Whiteboard is not limited to a specific industry or function—it can be used by a wide range of professionals, educators, and creatives.

For Businesses and Teams

1. Brainstorming Sessions – Teams can map out ideas visually, organize thoughts, and develop action plans.

2. Project Planning – Whiteboards allow teams to create project roadmaps, assign tasks, and track progress.

3. Agile and Scrum Workflows – Zoom Whiteboard can be used for Kanban boards, sprint planning, and backlog refinement in agile teams.

For Educators and Trainers

1. Interactive Teaching – Teachers can use the whiteboard to explain concepts, illustrate ideas, and encourage student participation.

2. Collaborative Learning – Students can work together on problems, share notes, and provide peer feedback.

3. Remote Workshops and Training – Instructors can create interactive lessons that keep learners engaged.

For Designers and Creatives

1. Wireframing and UI/UX Design – Zoom Whiteboard can be used for sketching layouts and planning user experiences.

2 Storyboarding – Teams can visualize storytelling elements for videos, animations, or marketing campaigns.

3 Brainstorming Mood Boards – Design teams can gather inspiration and explore **visual** themes collaboratively.

Seamless Integration with Zoom Workplace

Unlike third-party whiteboarding tools, Zoom Whiteboard is natively integrated within Zoom, making it more convenient for users who already rely on Zoom for meetings and communication.

Smooth Transition Between Meetings and Whiteboards

1 You can start a whiteboard during a Zoom meeting, allowing participants to contribute in real-time.

2 The whiteboard remains accessible even after the meeting ends, enabling teams to continue working asynchronously.

Cross-Platform Accessibility

1 Zoom Whiteboard can be accessed from desktop, mobile, and tablet devices, ensuring that users can contribute from anywhere.

2 Cloud-based storage allows users to save and revisit whiteboards without worrying about local storage limitations.

Integration with Other Zoom Features

- Combine Zoom Whiteboard with Zoom Chat to discuss ideas while collaborating.
- Use Zoom Breakout Rooms with separate whiteboards for small group discussions.
- Export whiteboards as PDFs or images for easy sharing and documentation.

Boosting Productivity with Advanced Features

Zoom Whiteboard is designed with features that help streamline workflows and increase productivity.

Pre-Built Templates for Quick Start

Instead of starting from scratch, users can choose from a variety of templates, such as:

- Brainstorming templates (e.g., mind maps, flowcharts)
- Project management templates (e.g., Kanban boards, Gantt charts)
- Business strategy templates (e.g., SWOT analysis, OKR tracking)

Smart Drawing and AI Assistance

- Zoom Whiteboard offers shape recognition, ensuring that hand-drawn circles, squares, and lines appear neatly.
- AI-powered suggestions can recommend layouts, connectors, and formatting improvements.

Easy Organization and Navigation

- Use layers to manage complex whiteboards efficiently.
- Zoom in and out to focus on different sections without losing context.
- Version history allows users to track changes and restore previous versions when needed.

Security and Collaboration Control

With increasing concerns over data privacy, Zoom Whiteboard incorporates security features to protect sensitive information.

Access Control and Permissions

- Admins can set user permissions, allowing for:
  - View-only access (for stakeholders who don't need to edit)
  - Edit access (for collaborators)
  - Comment-only mode (for feedback without modifications)
- Users can restrict who can share, edit, and download whiteboards.

Enterprise-Grade Security

- End-to-end encryption ensures that whiteboard data is secure.

- Compliance with industry standards such as GDPR, HIPAA, and SOC 2.

- Audit logs track who accesses and edits whiteboards for accountability.

Why Zoom Whiteboard Stands Out from Other Tools

While other digital whiteboard tools exist (e.g., Miro, Microsoft Whiteboard, Jamboard), Zoom Whiteboard offers unique advantages:

Feature	Zoom Whiteboard	Miro	Microsoft Whiteboard	Jamboard
Native Zoom Integration	✓ Yes	✗ No	✗ No	✗ No
Real-Time Collaboration	✓ Yes	✓ Yes	✓ Yes	✓ Yes
Cloud-Based Storage	✓ Yes	✓ Yes	✓ Yes	✓ Yes
Pre-Built Templates	✓ Yes	✓ Yes	✗ No	✗ No
Security & Compliance	✓ Yes	✓ Yes	✓ Yes	✗ No

The Zoom Advantage

- No need for extra logins or software installations—works within Zoom.

- Easier adoption for organizations already using Zoom Workplace.

- Tighter security measures compared to some third-party tools.

Conclusion

Zoom Whiteboard is a powerful, flexible, and secure tool that enhances virtual collaboration for businesses, educators, and creatives. Its deep integration with Zoom, real-time interaction capabilities, and productivity-boosting features make it an ideal choice for anyone looking to work smarter and more visually.

1.3 Key Features and Benefits

 Brainstorming & Ideation   Presenting & Teaching    Meetings & Workshops

Leverage Zoom's Existing Platform

Zoom's existing platform integrates perfectly with Zoom Whiteboard giving everyday Zoom users a whole new tool and a huge advantage when collaborating.

- Share or create real-time interactive whiteboards in Zoom Meetings. Give users different access depending on the meeting you are running.
- Take your workshops to the next level by offering whole new ways to work together using all of what Zoom has to offer.

1.3.1 Real-Time Collaboration

Introduction to Real-Time Collaboration

One of the most powerful features of Zoom Whiteboard is its ability to facilitate real-time collaboration. Whether you're working with a remote team, conducting an online workshop, teaching a virtual class, or brainstorming with colleagues, Zoom Whiteboard allows multiple users to contribute simultaneously. This seamless interaction fosters creativity, improves productivity, and enhances engagement, making it an essential tool for modern digital collaboration.

In this section, we will explore how real-time collaboration works, its benefits, best practices, and practical applications across various industries.

How Real-Time Collaboration Works in Zoom Whiteboard

Zoom Whiteboard is a cloud-based digital whiteboard that allows multiple users to interact simultaneously. This means that as one participant draws, adds notes, or moves elements, others can see these changes instantly. Here's how real-time collaboration works:

- **Multiple Participants Can Edit Simultaneously**

  - Zoom Whiteboard allows unlimited users (depending on your Zoom plan) to collaborate at the same time.

  - Changes made by one user appear instantly for all other participants.

  - Each participant's cursor is visible, showing who is making changes.

- **Live Sync Across Devices**

  - Whether you're on a computer, tablet, or mobile device, updates are synced in real time.

  - This ensures a seamless experience, allowing users to contribute from anywhere.

- **User Permissions and Roles**

  - The whiteboard owner or host can control who can edit, view, or comment.

  - Permissions can be set to "View Only," "Comment Only," or "Edit" to manage access levels.

  - This helps maintain organization and prevents unwanted changes.

- **Instant Feedback and Comments**

  - Users can leave sticky notes, comments, or annotations on any part of the board.

  - This feature allows teams to provide instant feedback, reducing the need for long email threads.

- **Integration with Zoom Meetings**

  - During a live Zoom call, participants can open and edit the Whiteboard together.

  - This enhances engagement and allows for real-time brainstorming, decision-making, and visual explanations.

- **Autosave and Version History**

  - Every change is automatically saved in the cloud.

○ Users can review past versions to track progress or undo mistakes.

Benefits of Real-Time Collaboration

1. Boosts Productivity and Efficiency

Instead of waiting for emails, downloading attachments, or merging feedback from multiple sources, users can work together instantly. This reduces delays and speeds up the decision-making process.

Example: In a project planning session, team members can simultaneously add tasks, assign responsibilities, and set deadlines directly on the Whiteboard without needing to email back and forth.

2. Enhances Creativity and Brainstorming

Real-time collaboration makes brainstorming sessions more dynamic. Instead of just discussing ideas verbally, participants can visualize concepts, sketch diagrams, and create flowcharts together.

Example: A marketing team can map out a campaign strategy, adding sticky notes for ideas and using connectors to structure a workflow—all in real time.

3. Improves Engagement and Teamwork

Participants feel more involved and engaged when they can actively contribute rather than just observe. This is particularly beneficial for remote teams and online classrooms.

Example: In a virtual class, students can solve math problems together, label diagrams, or complete group assignments in real time.

4. Enables Seamless Remote Work

With distributed teams becoming the norm, real-time collaboration in Zoom Whiteboard eliminates geographical barriers. Team members from different locations can work together as if they were in the same room.

Example: A software development team in different time zones can collaborate on a feature design, using sticky notes for feedback and drawing mockups together.

5. Reduces Miscommunication

Visual collaboration ensures everyone is on the same page. Instead of explaining complex ideas through text, teams can use diagrams, sketches, and annotations to communicate more effectively.

Example: A manager can illustrate a workflow process with arrows and labels, ensuring clarity for all team members.

6. Encourages Iteration and Refinement

Since changes are instant and not permanent, teams can experiment with ideas and quickly adjust their plans without worrying about losing data.

Example: A product design team can sketch multiple versions of a prototype, get feedback in real time, and refine their designs immediately.

Best Practices for Effective Real-Time Collaboration

1. Set Clear Objectives

Before starting a session, define the goal of the collaboration to keep discussions focused.

Example: If the goal is brainstorming marketing strategies, create designated areas on the Whiteboard for different campaign ideas.

2. Assign Roles and Responsibilities

To avoid confusion, assign specific roles such as:

- Facilitator: Guides the discussion and keeps the session on track.
- Note-Taker: Adds key points and action items.
- Designer: Organizes elements and structures the board.

3. Use Templates for Faster Workflows

Instead of starting from scratch, use pre-built templates for common tasks like:

- SWOT analysis
- Mind mapping
- Kanban boards

4. Enable Permissions Wisely

Control access settings to prevent accidental changes. If only a few people need to edit, set others to "View Only" mode.

5. Keep Whiteboards Organized

- Use color-coded sticky notes to differentiate topics.

- Group related elements together.

- Use titles and labels to make content easy to navigate.

6. Encourage Active Participation

Ask all participants to contribute ideas rather than just observing. Use polls, voting tools, or breakout groups to make collaboration more interactive.

Real-World Applications of Real-Time Collaboration

1. Business Meetings and Planning

- Project teams can create roadmaps, set goals, and track progress in real time.

- Leaders can visualize company strategies and collect feedback instantly.

2. Education and Training

- Teachers can create interactive lessons where students participate in solving problems.

- Online training sessions can include real-time diagrams and annotations to explain concepts clearly.

3. Product Design and Development

- Designers can collaborate on wireframes and iterate designs in real time.

- Engineers can sketch technical diagrams and make adjustments based on live input.

4. Marketing and Creative Workflows

- Teams can plan social media campaigns with interactive mood boards.

- Content creators can brainstorm article topics and visual elements together.

Conclusion

Real-time collaboration in Zoom Whiteboard is a game-changer for remote teams, educators, designers, and business professionals. By allowing multiple users to contribute simultaneously, providing instant updates, and integrating seamlessly with Zoom Meetings, it significantly enhances productivity, teamwork, and creative workflows.

By mastering this feature, you can transform the way you brainstorm, plan, and execute ideas, making collaboration more engaging and efficient than ever before.

1.3.2 Integration with Zoom Meetings and Workplace

Introduction

One of the most powerful aspects of Zoom Whiteboard is its seamless integration with Zoom Meetings and Zoom Workplace. This integration allows teams to collaborate in real time, brainstorm ideas, and visualize concepts without needing third-party tools. By embedding Zoom Whiteboard directly into Zoom Meetings and Workplace, users can enhance engagement, improve workflow efficiency, and foster creativity within their teams.

In this section, we will explore how Zoom Whiteboard integrates with Zoom Meetings and Workplace, its practical applications, benefits, and tips for maximizing its potential.

1. How Zoom Whiteboard Works with Zoom Meetings

Opening Zoom Whiteboard During a Meeting

When you are in a Zoom Meeting, you can easily launch **Zoom Whiteboard** without disrupting the flow of your discussion. Here's how:

- Start or Join a Zoom Meeting – Ensure you have host or co-host privileges to enable Whiteboard.

- Click on the "Whiteboard" Button – This is found in the meeting toolbar.

- Choose an Existing Whiteboard or Create a New One – You can continue working on a saved Whiteboard or start fresh.

- Collaborate in Real Time – All participants with permission can draw, annotate, and contribute instantly.

This feature is particularly useful for brainstorming sessions, problem-solving discussions, and interactive team meetings.

Sharing Whiteboard with Participants

Zoom Whiteboard allows different levels of access for participants. You can choose to:

- Allow everyone to edit – Best for brainstorming sessions and collaborative work.

- Restrict editing to specific users – Useful for structured meetings where only a few people need to contribute.

- View-only mode – Perfect for presentations or training sessions where you want to control the content.

These options ensure that your meetings remain organized and productive while maintaining control over the content.

Saving and Continuing Whiteboard Work Post-Meeting

A major advantage of integrating Zoom Whiteboard with Meetings is that work doesn't have to end when the meeting does. Users can:

- Save the Whiteboard automatically to Zoom Cloud or download it as an image/PDF.

- Access the same Whiteboard after the meeting via the Zoom Web Portal.

- Continue working on it asynchronously, ensuring a smooth workflow beyond live meetings.

This feature ensures that team members can revisit, refine, and implement ideas generated during meetings.

2. How Zoom Whiteboard Enhances Zoom Workplace

What is Zoom Workplace?

Zoom Workplace is an integrated platform within the Zoom ecosystem that allows teams to collaborate efficiently across different tools, including Meetings, Chat, Calendar, Email, and Whiteboard.

By integrating Zoom Whiteboard with Zoom Workplace, organizations can:

1. Streamline visual collaboration across different projects.

2. Use Whiteboards across multiple meetings without recreating content.

3. Enhance team coordination through persistent, accessible visual workspaces.

Using Zoom Whiteboard in Zoom Chat and Workspaces

Beyond meetings, Zoom Whiteboard can be shared and accessed through Zoom Chat and Workspaces:

- Attach a Whiteboard to a Zoom Chat Thread – Ideal for ongoing discussions and remote teamwork.

- Create a Whiteboard in a Zoom Workspace – Enables centralized collaboration where team members can edit and contribute at any time.

- Receive Notifications on Updates – If someone modifies a Whiteboard, members get updates, ensuring progress without needing additional meetings.

This makes Zoom Workplace a hub for continuous collaboration, keeping ideas and discussions accessible.

Integrating Zoom Whiteboard with Other Workplace Tools

In addition to Zoom's native tools, Whiteboard can also integrate with:

- Google Drive and Microsoft OneDrive – Store, share, and retrieve Whiteboards from cloud platforms.

- Slack and Microsoft Teams – Share Whiteboard links directly in team chats for cross-platform accessibility.

- Project Management Software (e.g., Trello, Asana, Monday.com) – Embed Whiteboards into task management platforms for better visualization of projects.

By extending beyond Zoom, Whiteboard becomes a powerful tool for company-wide collaboration, enhancing efficiency across different platforms.

3. Key Benefits of Zoom Whiteboard Integration

Increased Engagement in Virtual Meetings

Traditional online meetings often suffer from passive participation, but Zoom Whiteboard transforms meetings into interactive sessions. Benefits include:

✅ Encourages real-time input – Users can visually contribute instead of just speaking.

✅ Enhances idea retention – Visual elements help participants grasp and remember key points.

✅ Breaks down complex topics – Diagrams and sketches simplify difficult concepts.

This results in more effective and engaging virtual meetings.

Seamless Cross-Team Collaboration

With Whiteboard integrated across Zoom Meetings and Workplace, teams can:

✓ Work synchronously or asynchronously on shared Whiteboards.

✓ Eliminate the need for multiple tools, reducing complexity.

✓ Keep all brainstorming and planning sessions in one place, improving workflow efficiency.

This is particularly useful for remote and hybrid teams needing centralized collaboration tools.

Time-Saving and Workflow Efficiency

Zoom Whiteboard removes the need for separate apps (like Miro, MURAL, or Jamboard) by embedding whiteboarding directly into Zoom's ecosystem. This results in:
☐ Faster meeting setups – No switching between tools.
🕯 Instant access to past Whiteboards – No need to manually import/export files.
🗀 Organized storage – Whiteboards are linked directly to related meetings.

By streamlining workflows, organizations save time and boost productivity.

Enhanced Remote Learning and Training

For educators, trainers, and facilitators, Zoom Whiteboard provides:
⚙ Live annotations for better explanations
📌 Breakout room compatibility for small-group exercises
᠊᠊᠊ Persistent learning resources that students can revisit

This ensures a more interactive and effective remote learning environment.

---

4. Best Practices for Maximizing Zoom Whiteboard Integration

To fully utilize Zoom Whiteboard in Meetings and Workplace, consider these best practices:

Use Pre-Built Templates for Efficiency

Instead of starting from scratch, leverage Zoom's built-in templates for:
✍ Meeting agendas
⚙ Brainstorming sessions
᠊᠊᠊ Project planning and timelines

This saves time and standardizes collaboration across teams.

Assign Whiteboard Roles for Better Collaboration

In structured meetings, define roles:

👤 Facilitator – Guides the discussion and organizes content.

🖋 Contributor – Adds visual elements and annotations.

📌 Reviewer – Provides feedback and finalizes ideas.

This ensures a well-organized Whiteboarding experience.

Keep Whiteboards Organized and Labeled

To prevent clutter:

✔ Name Whiteboards based on topics or projects.

✔ Use layers and color coding to separate ideas.

✔ Archive old Whiteboards to avoid unnecessary duplication.

This improves searchability and efficiency.

Conclusion

The integration of Zoom Whiteboard with Zoom Meetings and Workplace transforms the way teams collaborate, brainstorm, and communicate. By embedding Whiteboarding features directly into live meetings, chat threads, and workspaces, Zoom provides a seamless, all-in-one platform for visual collaboration.

With proper usage, teams can boost engagement, streamline workflows, and enhance productivity—making Zoom Whiteboard a must-have tool for modern digital workplaces.

1.3.3 Templates and Customization Options

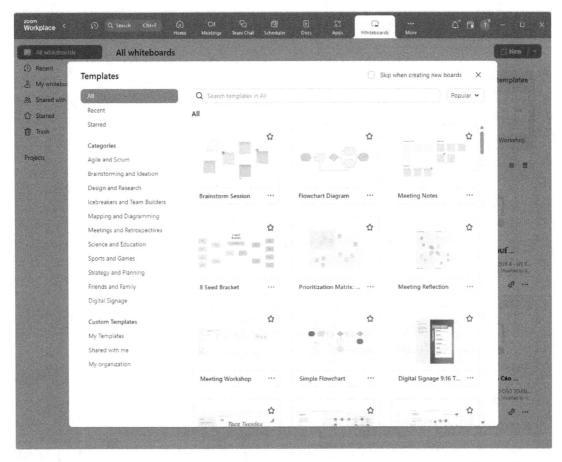

Zoom Whiteboard offers a variety of templates and customization options that make it a powerful tool for collaboration, brainstorming, and project planning. These features allow users to streamline their workflows, maintain consistency, and enhance productivity by using pre-designed templates or creating custom layouts suited to their specific needs.

In this section, we will explore:

- The importance of templates in digital whiteboarding.

- Built-in templates available in Zoom Whiteboard.

- Customizing templates to fit unique use cases.

- Saving and sharing custom templates for team collaboration.

- Best practices for using templates effectively.

Understanding the Role of Templates in Zoom Whiteboard

Templates serve as **pre-built structures** that provide a foundation for organizing ideas, planning projects, and visualizing data. Instead of starting from scratch, users can choose from a variety of ready-made templates that suit different business, education, and creative needs.

Benefits of Using Templates

1. **Saves Time:**

   o Templates eliminate the need to build whiteboards from the ground up, allowing users to focus on content rather than formatting.

2. **Ensures Consistency:**

   o Teams can maintain a uniform structure across different projects, ensuring everyone follows the same workflow.

3. **Enhances Collaboration:**

   o Predefined templates help groups quickly align on tasks, making meetings and brainstorming sessions more productive.

4. **Simplifies Complex Processes:**

   o Workflows such as project tracking, SWOT analysis, or customer journey mapping become **easier to manage** when using structured templates.

Built-in Templates in Zoom Whiteboard

Zoom Whiteboard comes with a library of pre-designed templates that cater to different use cases. These templates are categorized into various sections, such as brainstorming, project planning, education, and business strategy.

Common Built-in Templates and Their Uses

1. **Brainstorming Templates:**

   o **Mind Map Template** – Helps visualize ideas and relationships between concepts.

- o **Idea Board** – A simple structure for capturing team suggestions and feedback.

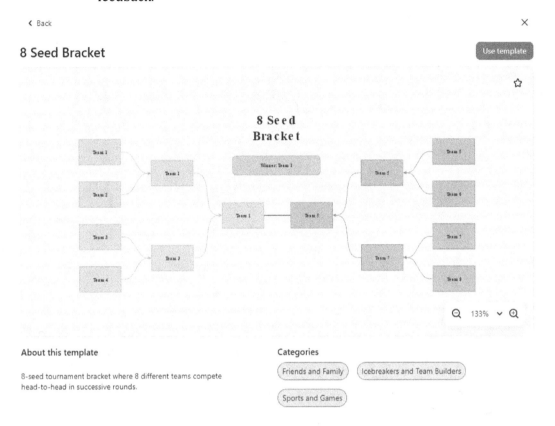

About this template

8-seed tournament bracket where 8 different teams compete head-to-head in successive rounds.

Categories

Friends and Family   Icebreakers and Team Builders

Sports and Games

2. **Project Planning Templates:**

- o **Kanban Board** – Organizes tasks into categories such as "To Do," "In Progress," and "Completed."

- o **Gantt Chart** – A timeline-based template for tracking project milestones and deadlines.

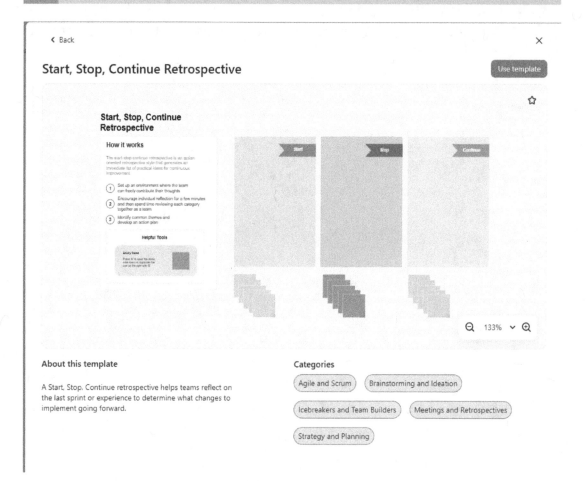

3. Education Templates:

- o **Lesson Plan Outline** – Provides a structure for teachers to design class materials.

- o **Venn Diagram** – Helps illustrate relationships and comparisons between different topics.

4. Business Strategy Templates:

- o **SWOT Analysis** – A structured format for identifying Strengths, Weaknesses, Opportunities, and Threats.

- o **Customer Journey Map** – Helps teams visualize a customer's experience with a product or service.

These templates **eliminate the need for repetitive formatting**, allowing users to focus on content and collaboration.

Customizing Templates in Zoom Whiteboard

While built-in templates provide a great starting point, customization allows users to tailor them to specific needs. Zoom Whiteboard offers various tools to modify templates, making them more relevant to your workflow.

Ways to Customize Templates

1. **Modifying Layouts and Sections:**
   - Users can resize, delete, or add sections to an existing template.
   - Adjusting layouts ensures the whiteboard structure aligns with team objectives.

2. **Changing Colors and Styles:**
   - Users can apply custom colors, fonts, and themes to personalize whiteboards.
   - This helps maintain branding consistency in business settings.

3. **Adding Interactive Elements:**
   - Embedding sticky notes, links, images, and videos enhances engagement.
   - Smart connectors can be used to link ideas visually for better organization.

4. **Using Layers for Better Organization:**
   - Layers allow users to group elements together, making it easier to navigate complex whiteboards.
   - This feature is especially useful for multi-stage planning or complex workflows.

Saving and Sharing Custom Templates

Once a user customizes a whiteboard layout, saving it as a reusable template can be a major time-saver. Zoom Whiteboard allows users to store templates in their library and share them with team members.

How to Save a Custom Template

1. Create a new whiteboard or modify an existing template.

2. Ensure all elements are properly organized.

3. Click on the "Save as Template" option.

4. Assign a name and category for easy identification.

5. Store it in the Zoom Whiteboard Library for future use.

Sharing Custom Templates with Teams

- **Internal Sharing:** Users can make their templates accessible to colleagues within the same Zoom Workplace account.

- **External Sharing:** Templates can be exported as PDFs or images for non-Zoom users.

- **Cloud Syncing:** Saved templates remain available across devices, ensuring seamless access during meetings or remote work sessions.

Best Practices for Using Templates Effectively

To maximize the benefits of Zoom Whiteboard templates, consider the following best practices:

1. Choose the Right Template for the Task

- Using a structured template aligned with the objective (e.g., project tracking, brainstorming, or presentations) ensures better results.

2. Keep the Template Simple and Clear

- Avoid cluttered layouts—too many elements can reduce readability and effectiveness.

3. Customize for Your Team's Needs

- Every team has unique requirements. Modify templates to match workflows and goals.

4. Use Templates as a Starting Point, Not a Limitation

- Templates should be flexible. Feel free to adapt and expand them based on evolving project needs.

5. Train Team Members on Template Usage

- Ensure that all participants understand how to use, edit, and contribute to shared templates.

Conclusion

Templates and customization options in Zoom Whiteboard are powerful tools that enhance collaboration and productivity. Whether you're using pre-built templates or creating custom layouts, these features allow for efficient organization, structured brainstorming, and effective communication. By leveraging Zoom Whiteboard's customization capabilities, teams can work smarter, stay organized, and unlock their creativity in virtual collaboration.

This section has provided a comprehensive guide on using templates in Zoom Whiteboard. In the next chapter, we will explore how to access and navigate the Zoom Whiteboard interface, ensuring a seamless user experience.

1.4 System Requirements and Setup

Zoom Whiteboard is a powerful digital collaboration tool that enhances teamwork, brainstorming, and visual thinking. Before diving into its features, it is essential to ensure that your system meets the necessary requirements and that you have correctly set up Zoom Whiteboard for optimal performance. This chapter will guide you through the system requirements and the setup process, ensuring a smooth experience.

System Requirements

Zoom Whiteboard is a cloud-based feature, which means it primarily runs on Zoom's online platform. However, depending on your device and operating system, certain technical requirements must be met to ensure a seamless experience.

Hardware Requirements

Your device must have sufficient processing power, memory, and internet capabilities to support Zoom Whiteboard efficiently. Below are the recommended hardware specifications:

- **For Desktops and Laptops (Windows & macOS)**
    - **Processor:** Minimum Intel i3 (Recommended Intel i5/i7 or AMD equivalent)
    - **RAM:** Minimum 4GB (Recommended 8GB or higher for smoother performance)
    - **Graphics Card:** Integrated GPU (Dedicated GPU recommended for heavy usage)
    - **Display Resolution:** Minimum 1024 x 768 (Recommended Full HD or higher)
    - **Internet Connection:** At least 5 Mbps for basic usage; 10 Mbps or higher for real-time collaboration with multiple users

- **For Tablets and Mobile Devices (iOS & Android)**
    - **Operating System:** iOS 12.0+ / Android 8.0+

- o **RAM:** Minimum 2GB (Recommended 4GB or higher)

- o **Processor:** A modern multi-core processor for smooth interactions

- o **Internet Connection:** Stable Wi-Fi or mobile data with at least 5 Mbps speed

Software Requirements

- **Operating System Compatibility:**

  - o Windows 10 or later (Windows 11 recommended)

  - o macOS 10.13 or later (macOS Ventura recommended)

  - o iOS 12.0 or later (for iPhones and iPads)

  - o Android 8.0 or later

- **Zoom Version Requirement:**

  - o Zoom Whiteboard is only available on **Zoom Workplace** with Zoom version **5.10.0 or later**. Users must ensure they have updated their Zoom application to access the feature.

- **Browser Support (For Web-Based Zoom Whiteboard):**

  - o Google Chrome (Recommended) – Latest version

  - o Microsoft Edge – Latest version

  - o Mozilla Firefox – Latest version

  - o Safari (for macOS users) – Latest version

Network and Security Requirements

Since Zoom Whiteboard is cloud-based, a **stable internet connection** is essential. Below are the recommended network settings:

- **Bandwidth:** At least **5 Mbps upload/download speed** for standard use; **10 Mbps or higher** for real-time collaboration with multiple participants.

- **Firewall Settings:** Ensure that Zoom domains (zoom.us, zoom.com) are **whitelisted** if you're using a corporate or educational network.

- **VPN Compatibility:** If you're using a Virtual Private Network (VPN), check that it allows Zoom services to function properly.

Setting Up Zoom Whiteboard

Once you have verified that your system meets the requirements, the next step is to set up Zoom Whiteboard. The process varies slightly based on whether you're using it on a desktop, web browser, or mobile device.

Enabling Zoom Whiteboard in Your Account

By default, Zoom Whiteboard should be available in Zoom Workplace. However, administrators may need to enable it for specific user groups or accounts.

For Individual Users:

1. Log in to your Zoom Web Portal (https://zoom.us/signin).

2. Navigate to Settings > Whiteboard.

3. Ensure that the Zoom Whiteboard toggle is enabled.

4. (Optional) Adjust permissions to allow sharing and collaboration with team members.

For Admins (Business & Enterprise Users):

1. Sign in to the Zoom Admin Portal.

2. Go to Account Settings > Whiteboard Management.

3. Toggle Enable Zoom Whiteboard for all users.

4. Configure access settings:

   o Allow users to create and edit whiteboards

   o Restrict whiteboard access to team members only

   o Set permissions for external collaborators

Accessing Zoom Whiteboard on Different Platforms

Once enabled, you can start using **Zoom Whiteboard** across multiple platforms.

1. Desktop App (Windows & macOS)

1. Open the Zoom Desktop Client.

2. Click on Whiteboard from the top navigation menu.

3. Select + New Whiteboard to start a fresh board.

4. To access saved whiteboards, go to Whiteboard Library.

2. Web Browser (Zoom Web Portal)

1. Open a browser and go to https://zoom.us/whiteboard.

2. Sign in with your Zoom account.

3. Click New Whiteboard to create a new board.

4. Browse your saved whiteboards in Recent Whiteboards.

3. Mobile App (iOS & Android)

1. Open the Zoom Mobile App.

2. Tap on Whiteboards from the bottom menu.

3. Select + New Whiteboard to start drawing.

4. Swipe left to see previously saved boards.

Customizing Your Whiteboard Settings

Once Zoom Whiteboard is set up, you may want to customize settings for a better experience.

Adjusting Default Permissions

- Navigate to Settings > Whiteboard Permissions
- Choose whether users can view, edit, or comment on shared whiteboards
- Enable automatic saving of whiteboards after meetings

Changing Whiteboard Display Preferences

- Toggle between light mode and dark mode
- Adjust canvas size to fit screen dimensions
- Enable gridlines for more precise drawing

Setting Up Templates for Quick Use

- Navigate to Whiteboard Templates
- Create custom layouts for meetings, brainstorming, project planning
- Save frequently used whiteboards for quick access

Troubleshooting Common Setup Issues

If you encounter issues while setting up Zoom Whiteboard, check the following:

Whiteboard Not Available in Zoom App

- Ensure you are using Zoom version 5.10.0 or later.
- Check that Whiteboard is enabled in account settings.

Unable to Save or Share Whiteboards

- Verify that cloud storage permissions are enabled.
- Ensure your organization's firewall settings allow Zoom services.

Slow Performance or Lag Issues

- Close unnecessary apps that consume system resources.

- Switch to a faster internet connection.

- Update graphics drivers and browser versions.

Final Thoughts on Setting Up Zoom Whiteboard

Once you have completed the setup, Zoom Whiteboard becomes a powerful tool for collaboration. Whether you are using it for team brainstorming, project planning, education, or design, ensuring your system meets the requirements and is properly configured will provide the best user experience.

Now that your Zoom Whiteboard is ready, let's move on to the next chapter to explore how to access and manage your whiteboards effectively.

◆ *Next: Chapter 2 - Getting Started with Zoom Whiteboard*

CHAPTER II
Getting Started with Zoom Whiteboard

2.1 How to Access Zoom Whiteboard

2.1.1 Using Zoom Web Portal

Zoom Whiteboard is a powerful tool that allows users to collaborate visually in real time. While it is seamlessly integrated into Zoom Meetings, users can also access and manage whiteboards independently through the **Zoom Web Portal**. This method is especially useful for preparing content before a meeting, organizing ideas, and reviewing whiteboards without needing to start a live session.

In this section, we will explore:

- How to log into the **Zoom Web Portal**
- How to navigate to the **Whiteboard section**
- Creating a new whiteboard
- Managing existing whiteboards
- Sharing and collaborating on whiteboards

1. Logging into the Zoom Web Portal

To access the Zoom Whiteboard through the web, follow these steps:

1. **Open Your Web Browser**

- o Zoom Whiteboard is available through the Zoom Web Portal and can be accessed from any modern web browser (Google Chrome, Microsoft Edge, Mozilla Firefox, or Safari).

- o Make sure your browser is updated to the latest version for the best performance.

2. **Go to the Zoom Web Portal**

- o In your browser, type **https://zoom.us** and press **Enter**.

- o This will take you to the official Zoom login page.

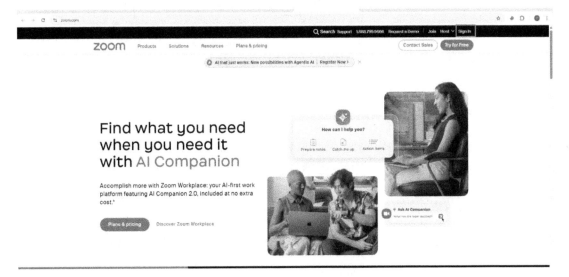

3. **Sign in to Your Zoom Account**

- o Click on Sign In at the top right corner.

- o Enter your email address and password associated with your Zoom account.

- o If you use SSO (Single Sign-On) or sign in via Google or Facebook, select the appropriate option.

- o If you do not have an account yet, click on Sign Up Free to create one.

4. **Navigate to the Whiteboard Section**

- o Once logged in, locate the **Whiteboard** option in the left-hand navigation panel.

- o Click on **Whiteboard** to enter the main whiteboard dashboard.

2. Navigating the Zoom Whiteboard Dashboard

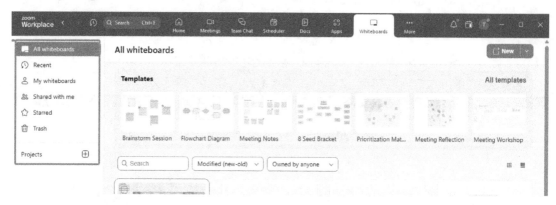

The Whiteboard Dashboard in the Zoom Web Portal is the central place where all your whiteboards are stored and managed. The dashboard is divided into different sections:

- **My Whiteboards** – Displays all whiteboards you have created or that have been shared with you.

- **Shared With Me** – Lists all whiteboards that other users have given you access to.

- **Recent Whiteboards** – Shows the most recently opened whiteboards for quick access.

- **Trash** – Contains deleted whiteboards that can be restored if needed.

At the top of the page, there are options to search for whiteboards, filter by date or owner, and create new whiteboards.

3. Creating a New Whiteboard

To create a new whiteboard through the **Zoom Web Portal**, follow these steps:

1. **Click on "New Whiteboard"**

o   On the Whiteboard Dashboard, look for the **"New Whiteboard"** button, usually located at the top right corner.

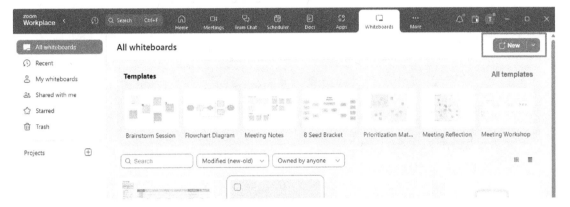

2. **Choose a Template or Start from Scratch**

    o   Zoom provides several built-in **templates** for brainstorming, project planning, and education.

    o   You can select a template or click **"Blank Whiteboard"** to start with a clean slate.

3. **Set Permissions and Access**

   o Before starting, you can adjust the **sharing settings**:

      ▪ Keep it **Restricted** (only you can access).

      ▪ Share with specific team members.

      ▪ Make it accessible to everyone in your organization.

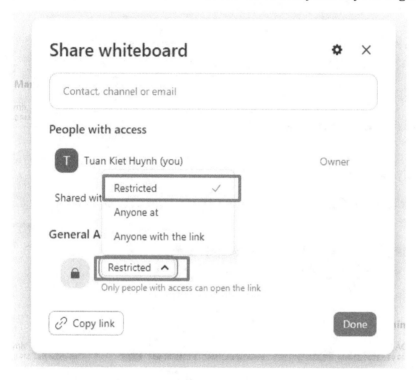

4. **Start Using the Whiteboard**

   o Once the whiteboard opens, you will have access to all drawing, annotation, and collaboration tools.

---

4. Managing Existing Whiteboards

Once you have created multiple whiteboards, it is essential to keep them organized. Here are some useful management features:

Organizing Your Whiteboards

- Rename Whiteboards – Click on the title of a whiteboard to rename it.

- Use Folders or Tags – Some Zoom versions allow you to categorize whiteboards for better organization.

- Archive Old Whiteboards – Instead of deleting, you can archive whiteboards that are not in active use.

Deleting and Restoring Whiteboards

- Move to Trash – If a whiteboard is no longer needed, click on the three-dot menu next to the file and select Delete.

- Restore from Trash – If you accidentally delete a whiteboard, go to the Trash section and restore it within 30 days before it is permanently removed.

5. Sharing and Collaborating on Whiteboards

One of the most powerful features of Zoom Whiteboard is its ability to collaborate with others in real time.

How to Share a Whiteboard

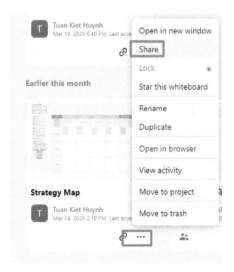

To share a whiteboard from the **Zoom Web Portal**:

1. Open the whiteboard you want to share.

2. Click the **Share** button at the top right corner.

3. Choose how you want to share:

    o **Invite specific people** – Enter their email addresses.

    o **Generate a link** – Create a shareable link with different access levels.

    o **Adjust permissions** – Choose whether participants can edit, comment, or view only.

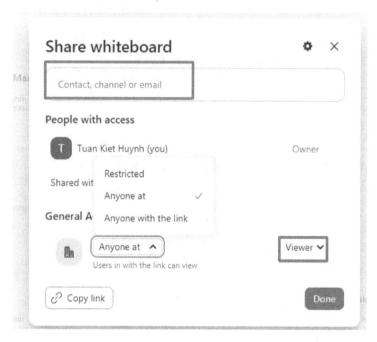

Collaborating in Real-Time

Once shared, team members can:

- Draw, annotate, and add sticky notes in real time.

- Comment on specific elements for feedback.

- Use version history to revert changes if needed.

Zoom Whiteboard supports simultaneous editing, making it ideal for team meetings, brainstorming sessions, and remote collaboration.

6. Advantages of Using the Web Portal for Zoom Whiteboard

Using the Zoom Web Portal for Whiteboard access has several benefits:

✅ No need to start a meeting – Work on whiteboards anytime.
✅ Easier management – Quickly find, edit, and organize whiteboards.
✅ Better collaboration – Share with others without opening a Zoom call.
✅ Cross-device accessibility – Use Zoom Whiteboard from a PC, laptop, or tablet.

7. Troubleshooting Common Issues

Even with a seamless interface, you may encounter occasional issues. Here's how to fix them:

Whiteboard Not Loading

◆ Check your internet connection.
◆ Clear your browser cache and restart.
◆ Ensure you have the latest version of Zoom.

Unable to Share Whiteboard

◆ Confirm that you have sharing permissions enabled.
◆ Check if your Zoom account type supports whiteboard sharing.

Whiteboard Changes Not Saving

◆ Ensure auto-save is enabled.
◆ Manually click Save before exiting.

Final Thoughts

Using the Zoom Web Portal to access Zoom Whiteboard offers flexibility and efficiency for both individual users and teams. By following this guide, you can effortlessly create, manage, and collaborate on whiteboards without needing a Zoom meeting.

In the next section, we will explore how to use Zoom Whiteboard in an active Zoom Meeting and make real-time collaboration even more interactive.

2.1.2 Opening Whiteboard in a Zoom Meeting

Zoom Whiteboard is a powerful feature that allows users to collaborate in real time, brainstorm ideas, and visualize concepts directly within a Zoom meeting. Whether you are a business professional, educator, or creative thinker, using Zoom Whiteboard effectively in meetings can enhance teamwork, improve communication, and make discussions more interactive.

In this section, we will walk you through the steps to open Zoom Whiteboard during a meeting, explain the different options available, and provide useful tips to maximize its potential.

1. Enabling Zoom Whiteboard Before a Meeting

Before you can use Zoom Whiteboard in a meeting, you need to ensure that the feature is enabled in your Zoom settings. If the option is not available, you may need to request access from your Zoom administrator (for business accounts) or enable it manually in your personal settings.

Checking Your Zoom Version

Zoom Whiteboard is a relatively new feature, and to access it, you must have an updated version of Zoom. Follow these steps to check and update your Zoom client:

1. Open the Zoom desktop client or mobile app.

2. Click on your profile picture in the top right corner.

3. Select Check for Updates.

4. If an update is available, install it and restart Zoom.

It is always recommended to keep Zoom updated to access the latest features and security improvements.

Enabling Zoom Whiteboard in Settings

To ensure that Zoom Whiteboard is available in your meetings, follow these steps:

1. **Log in** to your Zoom account at zoom.us.

2. Click on **Settings** in the left-hand menu.

3. Under the **Meeting** tab, scroll down to find **Zoom Whiteboard**.

4. Toggle the switch to **enable** the feature.

5. (Optional) If you are an admin, you can enable **Whiteboard Cloud Storage** to allow saving and sharing across meetings.

Once enabled, you will see the Whiteboard option available inside your Zoom meetings.

2. Opening Zoom Whiteboard During a Meeting

Once you have enabled Zoom Whiteboard, you can access it easily during a live Zoom meeting. Below are the step-by-step instructions for opening a whiteboard on desktop, mobile, and web versions of Zoom.

2.1 Opening Zoom Whiteboard on Desktop (Windows & macOS)

1. Start or join a Zoom meeting.

2. In the meeting toolbar at the bottom, click on Whiteboards.

3. Select New Whiteboard to create a fresh whiteboard or choose from a previously saved whiteboard.

4. The Zoom Whiteboard interface will open, allowing you to start drawing, adding text, and collaborating with participants.

2.2 Opening Zoom Whiteboard on Mobile (iOS & Android)

1. Open the Zoom mobile app and join a meeting.

2. Tap on the More (…) button at the bottom right.

3. Select Whiteboards from the menu.

4. Tap New Whiteboard to start a blank whiteboard or open an existing one.

5. Use the touch-friendly drawing tools to annotate and collaborate.

2.3 Opening Zoom Whiteboard on Web (Browser Version)

1. Start or join a Zoom meeting from your web browser.

2. Click on the More options button in the meeting controls.

3. Select Whiteboards from the drop-down menu.

4. Choose New Whiteboard to begin or select an existing one from your library.

The web version provides a slightly limited experience compared to the desktop app, but it still allows basic drawing, text input, and collaboration.

---

3. Using Zoom Whiteboard in a Meeting

Once your whiteboard is open, you can use it in various ways to enhance communication and collaboration.

3.1 Navigating the Whiteboard Interface

When you open a whiteboard in a Zoom meeting, you will see a set of tools and options, including:

- Drawing tools (pen, highlighter, shapes)
- Text input for adding typed notes
- Sticky notes for organizing ideas
- Image and PDF upload to annotate documents
- Smart connectors to link ideas together
- Collaboration settings to allow or restrict editing

3.2 Sharing the Whiteboard with Participants

By default, only the meeting host or designated co-hosts can create and manage whiteboards. However, you can enable collaboration by following these steps:

1. Click on the Share button in the Whiteboard toolbar.
2. Choose Who can edit (Only me, Everyone, or Specific people).
3. Send invitations or generate a sharing link for external users.

Allowing all participants to edit in real time can be useful for brainstorming sessions, group projects, and interactive training.

3.3 Using Whiteboard with Breakout Rooms

If your Zoom meeting includes **Breakout Rooms**, you can assign whiteboards to specific groups. Here's how:

1. Open the Breakout Rooms panel.
2. Assign participants to rooms as needed.
3. Instruct each group to open a New Whiteboard in their room.
4. After the breakout session, all whiteboards can be merged into the main room for discussion.

Breakout Room whiteboards are a great way to facilitate teamwork and structured discussions.

4. Tips for Maximizing Whiteboard Usage in Meetings

To get the most out of Zoom Whiteboard during meetings, consider these best practices:

Plan Ahead

- Set up your whiteboards before the meeting and save templates for quick access.
- Use predefined layouts to structure discussions.

Use Annotation Tools Effectively

- Use different colors and line thicknesses to differentiate ideas.
- Highlight key points using the highlighter tool.

Encourage Participant Engagement

- Assign specific roles (e.g., a note-taker or facilitator).
- Enable sticky notes for quick brainstorming sessions.

Save and Export Your Whiteboards

- Always save your whiteboards after the meeting for future reference.
- Export whiteboards as PDFs or images for easy sharing.

5. Troubleshooting Common Issues

Even though Zoom Whiteboard is easy to use, users may sometimes encounter issues. Below are some common problems and how to fix them:

Whiteboard Option Not Available

- Ensure Zoom Whiteboard is **enabled** in your account settings.
- Update your Zoom client to the latest version.

Participants Cannot Edit the Whiteboard

- Check collaboration settings under **Who can edit**.
- Ensure participants are using a compatible Zoom version.

Whiteboard Not Saving or Syncing

- Check your **Zoom cloud storage** settings.

- Ensure you have a **stable internet connection**.

Conclusion

Opening and using Zoom Whiteboard in a meeting is a straightforward process, but mastering its features can greatly improve your productivity and collaboration. By enabling Whiteboard in your settings, learning to navigate its tools, and implementing best practices, you can create more engaging and interactive Zoom sessions.

In the next section, we will explore **how to create and manage whiteboards effectively**, including saving, organizing, and sharing them for long-term use.

2.1.3 Accessing Whiteboard on Mobile Devices

Zoom Whiteboard is a powerful collaboration tool that allows users to brainstorm, illustrate concepts, and engage with teams remotely. While most users access it through the desktop app or web portal, Zoom Whiteboard is also available on mobile devices, making it convenient for users who are on the go. Whether you're using a smartphone or tablet, you can access, create, and edit whiteboards from anywhere with an internet connection.

In this section, we will explore how to access Zoom Whiteboard on iOS and Android devices, discuss the interface differences compared to desktop versions, and highlight best practices for mobile collaboration.

Zoom Whiteboard Availability on Mobile

Before diving into the steps to access Zoom Whiteboard on mobile devices, it's essential to understand its availability and compatibility:

- Supported Devices: Zoom Whiteboard is accessible on both iOS and Android devices, including smartphones and tablets.

- Zoom App Requirement: Users must have the latest version of the Zoom mobile app installed. Older versions may not support Whiteboard features.

- Feature Limitations: While most core functionalities are available, some advanced tools (such as certain integrations and complex formatting options) may be limited on mobile compared to desktop.

To ensure the best experience, always update the Zoom app to the latest version from the Apple App Store (iOS) or Google Play Store (Android).

How to Access Zoom Whiteboard on Mobile

There are two primary ways to access Zoom Whiteboard on a mobile device:

1. Through the Zoom App (Standalone Whiteboard Access)
2. During an Ongoing Zoom Meeting

Let's explore each method in detail.

1. Accessing Zoom Whiteboard from the Zoom App

If you want to use Zoom Whiteboard outside of a meeting—such as for brainstorming, planning, or personal note-taking—you can access it directly from the Zoom app.

Steps to Access:

1. **Open the Zoom app** on your mobile device.
2. Tap on the **"Whiteboards"** tab at the bottom navigation bar.
   - If you don't see this tab, ensure your app is updated to the latest version.
3. Tap **"+" (Create New Whiteboard)** to start a new whiteboard.
4. If you want to access an existing whiteboard:
   - Scroll through your list of saved whiteboards, or
   - Use the **search bar** to find a specific one.
5. Tap on the whiteboard to open and start editing.

Key Features Available on Mobile:

- Basic drawing and annotation tools (pen, highlighter, shapes)
- Adding text boxes and sticky notes

- Zoom in/out gestures for better navigation

- Sharing whiteboards with collaborators

2. Accessing Zoom Whiteboard During a Meeting

If you need to use Whiteboard as part of a Zoom meeting, you can do so directly within the call.

Steps to Use Whiteboard in a Meeting:

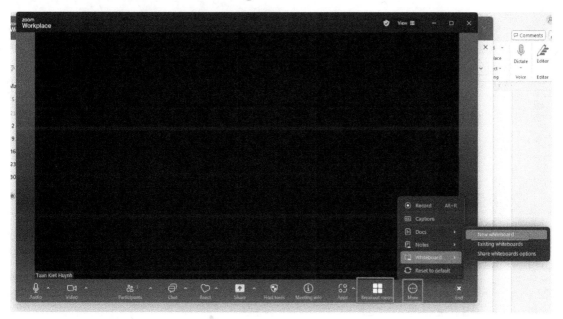

1. Join or Start a Zoom Meeting on your mobile device.

2. Tap on the "More" button (three dots) in the bottom-right corner of the meeting toolbar.

3. Select "Whiteboard" from the menu.

4. Choose "New Whiteboard" to create a fresh canvas or open an existing one.

5. Once the whiteboard is open, you can:

    o   Draw and annotate using the mobile tools.

    o   Collaborate with participants in real time.

o   Allow others to edit or restrict them to viewing only.

Note: The Whiteboard will remain **available even after the meeting ends**, so participants can revisit or continue editing later.

Understanding the Mobile Whiteboard Interface

The mobile version of Zoom Whiteboard is optimized for touchscreen interactions. Here's what you need to know:

Toolbar Overview (Mobile Interface)

Unlike the desktop version, the mobile interface has a **compact and simplified toolbar** at the bottom of the screen, which includes:

- **Pen Tool**: For freehand drawing and annotations.

- **Highlighter Tool**: To emphasize certain areas on the board.

- **Shapes and Lines**: For creating structured visuals.

- **Text Tool**: Adding labels, explanations, or titles.

- **Sticky Notes**: Quick notes for brainstorming sessions.

- **Eraser Tool**: To remove unwanted markings.

Navigation & Zooming:

- Use **pinch-to-zoom** gestures to move across the whiteboard.

- Drag with two fingers to **pan across large whiteboards**.

Tips for Using Zoom Whiteboard Effectively on Mobile

To enhance your experience using Zoom Whiteboard on a mobile device, consider the following best practices:

✓ **Use a Stylus for Precision** – If your device supports a stylus (e.g., Apple Pencil, Samsung S Pen), it can provide greater accuracy when drawing or writing.

✓ **Leverage Voice-to-Text for Faster Notes** – Instead of typing, use your device's voice-to-text feature to quickly create text annotations.

✓ **Rotate Your Screen for More Space** – Using your device in landscape mode provides a larger workspace.

✓ **Save and Sync Across Devices** – Since Whiteboards are stored in the cloud, you can start a whiteboard on mobile and continue editing on your desktop later.

✓ **Manage Permissions Carefully** – Before sharing a whiteboard, control editing permissions to avoid accidental modifications.

Common Issues and Troubleshooting

While Zoom Whiteboard works seamlessly on mobile devices, you may encounter occasional issues. Below are some common problems and how to fix them:

◆ Whiteboard Tab Missing

- Ensure your Zoom app is updated to the latest version.

- Check your Zoom account settings to verify that the Whiteboard feature is enabled.

◆ Lag or Slow Performance

- Close other background apps to free up memory.

- Switch to a stronger Wi-Fi connection if possible.

◆ Can't Save Whiteboard Changes

- Ensure your internet connection is stable.

- Check if you have editing permissions (if collaborating on a shared whiteboard).

◆ Lost Whiteboard Progress

- Open Version History to see if an earlier version was saved automatically.

- If Whiteboard was shared in a meeting, ask the host to re-enable access.

Conclusion

Accessing Zoom Whiteboard on mobile devices allows users to collaborate anytime, anywhere, making it a highly flexible tool for business meetings, remote learning, and creative projects. While it offers a slightly simplified interface compared to the desktop version, its core features remain powerful enough for effective collaboration. By understanding how to navigate the interface, use essential tools, and troubleshoot common issues, users can maximize their productivity on the go.

In the next section, we will explore how to create and manage whiteboards efficiently, ensuring that your work remains organized and accessible across all devices.

2.2 Creating and Managing Whiteboards

2.2.1 Starting a New Whiteboard

Introduction

Starting a new whiteboard in Zoom Whiteboard is the first step toward unlocking the full potential of digital collaboration. Whether you are brainstorming ideas, planning a project, or teaching a class, Zoom Whiteboard provides an intuitive and flexible environment for creating and sharing visual content.

This section will guide you through the process of starting a new whiteboard, covering different access methods, key interface elements, and essential settings to help you get started smoothly.

1. Accessing Zoom Whiteboard

Before you can create a new whiteboard, you need to know where and how to access the Zoom Whiteboard feature. Zoom offers multiple ways to access Whiteboard, depending on your workflow:

Using the Zoom Web Portal

The Zoom Web Portal is the primary way to create and manage whiteboards outside of Zoom meetings. Follow these steps to start a whiteboard:

1. **Go to the Zoom Web Portal:** Open your web browser and navigate to https://zoom.us.

2. **Sign in to your Zoom account:** Use your credentials to log in. Ensure that your account has the Whiteboard feature enabled.

3. **Access the Whiteboard Section:**

   o   In the left-side navigation panel, click on **"Whiteboard"**.

   o   Here, you will see a list of existing whiteboards, as well as an option to create a new one.

4. **Click on "New Whiteboard":** This opens a blank workspace where you can start adding content immediately.

5. **Customize your Whiteboard settings:** You can adjust settings such as privacy, access permissions, and sharing options before inviting collaborators.

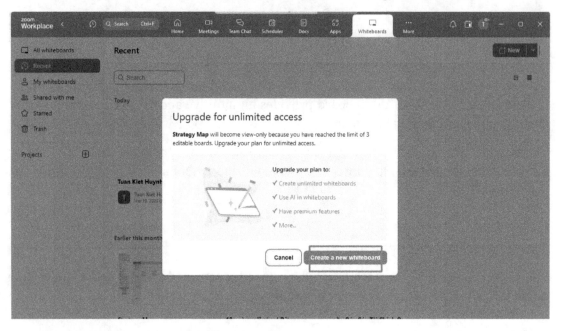

Starting a Whiteboard in a Zoom Meeting

If you want to create a whiteboard during a live Zoom meeting, follow these steps:

1. **Start or Join a Zoom Meeting:** Open Zoom and either create a new meeting or join an existing one.

2. **Click on the Whiteboard Icon:**

    o   In the Zoom meeting toolbar, click on the **"Whiteboard"** button.

    o   If you don't see it, click on **"More"** (three dots) to find additional tools.

3. **Choose "New Whiteboard":** Zoom will launch a fresh whiteboard, and all participants with editing access can contribute.

4. **Adjust Whiteboard Permissions:**

- o By default, all meeting participants can view the whiteboard.

- o To restrict editing, click on the **"Share"** button and modify participant permissions.

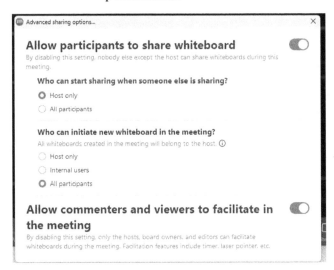

Accessing Zoom Whiteboard on Mobile Devices

If you're using Zoom on an iPad, iPhone, or Android device, you can still start a new whiteboard:

1. Open the Zoom App: Make sure you have the latest version of the Zoom app installed.

2. Start or Join a Meeting: The whiteboard feature is available only in meetings.

3. Tap the "Share" Button: Unlike the desktop version, the whiteboard tool is found under "Share Content".

4. Select "Whiteboard" from the List: This will launch a new whiteboard that you can edit using your touchscreen.

5. Use Drawing Tools: On mobile, you can use pen, highlighter, eraser, and shape tools with your finger or a stylus.

2. Understanding the Zoom Whiteboard Interface

Once you have created a new whiteboard, you will see a blank workspace with several tools and options. Here's what you need to know:

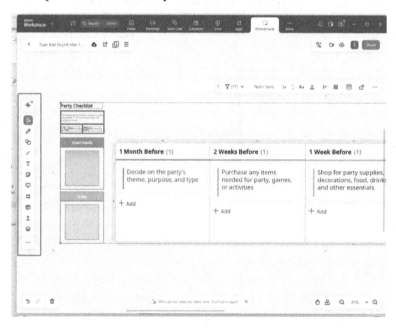

The Toolbar

The toolbar provides all the tools you need to create and edit content:

- Pen Tool: Freehand drawing for sketches or quick notes.

- Text Tool: Add typed text anywhere on the whiteboard.

- Shapes and Lines: Insert pre-made shapes like rectangles, circles, and arrows.

- Sticky Notes: Add color-coded notes for brainstorming sessions.

- Eraser: Remove unwanted elements with a single click.

- Undo/Redo Buttons: Quickly revert or reapply actions.

The Canvas

The main whiteboard workspace where you can draw, type, and insert images. The infinite canvas feature lets you scroll and expand your workspace without limits.

The Sharing and Collaboration Panel

This section allows you to:

- Invite others to view or edit the whiteboard.

- Control participant permissions (view-only, comment, or full edit).

- Save or export the whiteboard for future use.

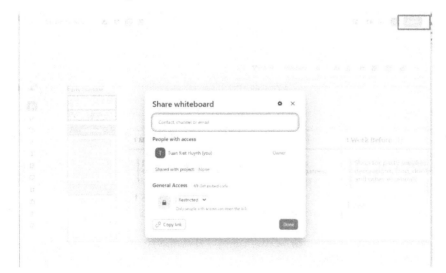

3. Customizing Your Whiteboard

Before you start working on your whiteboard, consider adjusting the following settings:

Choosing a Background

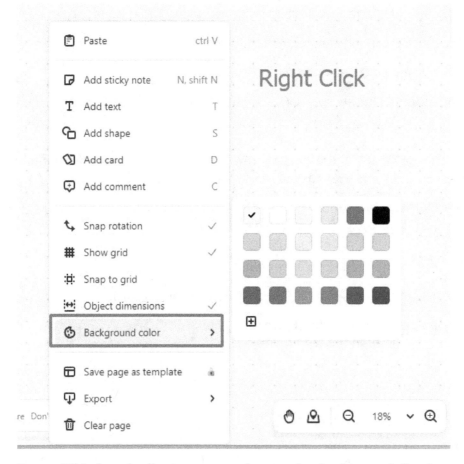

Zoom Whiteboard allows you to change the background for better visibility and organization. Options include:

- Plain White: Standard whiteboard experience.

- Grid Lines: Ideal for technical drawings and diagrams.

- Dark Mode: A high-contrast mode for reducing eye strain.

To change the background:

1. Right + Click and chose the **"Background color"** option.

2. Select your preferred background style.

Adjusting Canvas Size

By default, Zoom Whiteboard has an infinite canvas, but you can adjust the visible area by:

- Zooming in and out using the zoom slider.

- Dragging the canvas to explore different areas.

Setting Up Permissions

If you're working in a team, it's important to configure sharing settings:

- Open the Share menu from the top-right corner.

- Choose who can access the whiteboard: Specific individuals, meeting participants, or anyone with the link.

- Set permission levels: View-only, Comment, or Edit.

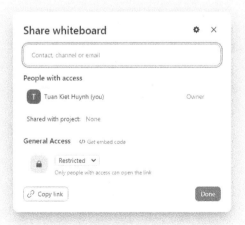

4. Saving and Exporting Your Whiteboard

Once you've started a whiteboard, you may need to save or export it for later use.

Saving Your Progress

All changes in Zoom Whiteboard are automatically saved to the cloud. However, you can manually:

- Click "Save" in the top-right corner.

- Rename your whiteboard for easy organization.

Exporting as an Image or PDF

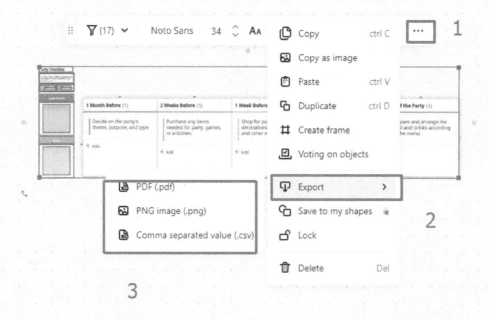

To share your whiteboard outside Zoom:

1. Click **"Export"** in the toolbar.

2. Choose **PNG, JPEG, or PDF** format.

3. Download the file or email it directly to team members.

5. Best Practices for Starting a Whiteboard

Here are some expert tips to ensure you start your whiteboard efficiently:

Plan Before You Start

- Outline your goals before creating the whiteboard.
- Use templates if applicable.

Use Colors and Labels

- Assign different colors for different ideas.
- Use labels and sticky notes for better organization.

Keep It Organized

- Group related elements using the layer and grouping tools.
- Use guidelines and grids to keep items aligned.

Conclusion

Starting a new whiteboard in Zoom Whiteboard is a simple yet powerful process. Whether you are accessing it from the web portal, a live Zoom meeting, or a mobile device, understanding the interface, tools, and customization options will help you create an engaging and productive workspace.

By mastering the toolbar, collaboration settings, and exporting options, you can ensure that your whiteboard sessions are efficient and effective. In the next section, we will dive deeper into saving, organizing, and sharing your whiteboards for seamless collaboration.

2.2.2 Saving and Organizing Whiteboards

Effective management of Zoom Whiteboards is crucial for seamless collaboration and productivity. Saving and organizing whiteboards ensures that your work remains accessible, structured, and easy to reference. This section will explore various methods to save your whiteboards, organize them efficiently, and implement best practices for maintaining a well-structured workspace.

1. Understanding How Zoom Whiteboards Are Saved

Zoom Whiteboard operates as a cloud-based tool, meaning that all whiteboards are automatically saved to your Zoom account unless manually deleted. Unlike traditional physical whiteboards, which disappear once erased, Zoom Whiteboard allows you to save, retrieve, and edit your work at any time.

By default, Zoom Whiteboards are stored in the Whiteboard Dashboard, accessible through the Zoom Web Portal or the Zoom Desktop and Mobile Apps. Understanding how Zoom manages whiteboards will help you avoid losing important work and streamline your workflow.

2. Saving Whiteboards in Zoom

Auto-Save Feature

One of the most convenient features of Zoom Whiteboard is auto-save. Every change made to a whiteboard is automatically saved in real-time. This eliminates the need for manual saving and ensures that all edits are preserved even if you accidentally close the whiteboard or lose internet connectivity.

However, while auto-save is helpful, it's still important to manually save and name your whiteboards to keep them organized.

Manually Saving a Whiteboard

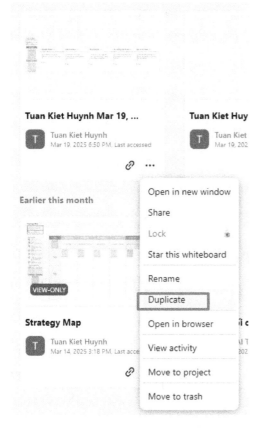

If you want to **manually save a specific version** of a whiteboard, follow these steps:

1. Open the **Zoom Whiteboard Dashboard**.

2. Locate the whiteboard you are currently working on.

3. Click on the **three-dot menu** next to the whiteboard's name.

4. Select **"Duplicate"** to create a backup copy.

5. Choose a specific folder or rename the whiteboard for clarity.

This ensures that even if you continue editing the whiteboard, you still have a saved version of the original state.

Exporting a Whiteboard as an Image or PDF

While Zoom Whiteboard is cloud-based, you may need to save a **static version** for offline access or sharing with external users. Zoom allows you to export whiteboards in various formats:

Steps to Export a Whiteboard:

1. Open the whiteboard you want to save.

2. Click the **export** icon (usually represented by a download or share button).

3. Choose the desired format:

     o **PNG** (for high-quality images)

     o **PDF** (for multi-page documents)

4. Select the preferred location on your device and save the file.

This method is especially useful for archiving old whiteboards, sharing finalized work with colleagues, or printing physical copies.

3. Organizing Whiteboards for Easy Access

Having multiple whiteboards can become overwhelming without proper organization. Zoom Whiteboard provides various tools to help users categorize, rename, and structure their workspaces efficiently.

Naming Conventions for Whiteboards

A clear naming system helps differentiate whiteboards, making it easier to locate them later. Consider the following best practices:

✓ Use Descriptive Titles: Instead of "Untitled Whiteboard 1," use "Marketing Brainstorm – Q1 2025."
✓ Include Dates in Names: Example: "Product Development_03-15-2025."
✓ Add Team or Project Labels: Example: "[HR] Employee Onboarding Plan."

You can rename a whiteboard anytime by:

1. Navigating to the Whiteboard Dashboard.

2. Clicking on the three-dot menu next to the whiteboard.

3. Selecting "Rename" and entering a new title.

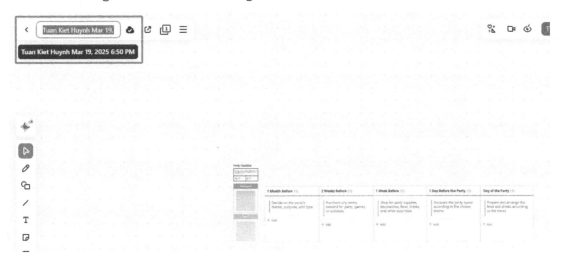

3.2 Using Folders to Categorize Whiteboards

Zoom Whiteboard allows users to **create folders** to group related whiteboards. This is especially useful for teams managing multiple projects.

How to Create and Use Folders:

1. Go to the **Whiteboard Dashboard**.

2. Click **"New Folder"** and enter a name.

3. Drag and drop existing whiteboards into the folder.

4. Share folders with specific team members to manage collaborative projects.

Example Folder Structures:

- 📁 **Marketing Campaigns**

  o Q1 Strategy Board

  o Social Media Content Plan

- 📁 **Project Management**

  o Sprint Planning

  o Budget Allocation

- 📁 **Training Materials**

  o Employee Handbook Overview

  o Onboarding Checklist

3.3 Deleting Whiteboards

How to Delete a Whiteboard Permanently:

1. Open the **Whiteboard Dashboard**.

2. Click on the **three-dot menu** next to the whiteboard.

3. Select **"Move to trash"** and confirm your choice.

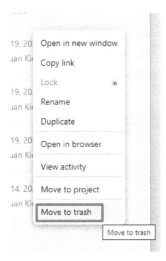

⚠ **Important:** Deleted whiteboards **cannot be recovered** unless previously exported or duplicated.

---

4. Best Practices for Managing Whiteboards

Regularly Review and Clean Up Whiteboards

Over time, you may accumulate numerous whiteboards. To avoid clutter:

- Set a monthly cleanup schedule.

- Delete or archive outdated whiteboards.

- Merge related whiteboards into larger project boards.

Assign Ownership and Access Permissions

If working in a team, it's essential to manage permissions properly. Zoom allows whiteboard owners to:

- Set view-only or edit access for collaborators.

- Restrict access to specific teams or individuals.

- Enable expiration dates for access links.

This prevents unauthorized edits and ensures that only relevant team members can modify content.

Back Up Important Whiteboards

Even though Zoom Whiteboard saves data automatically, it's a good practice to create backups:

- Export critical whiteboards as PDFs.

- Save high-priority boards in a dedicated "Important Documents" folder.

- Use Zoom integrations with cloud storage solutions like Google Drive or Dropbox for additional backups.

---

5. Conclusion: Maintaining an Organized Whiteboard Workspace

Saving and organizing Zoom Whiteboards is essential for maximizing productivity and collaboration. By following structured naming conventions, categorization methods, and best practices, users can maintain a clean, efficient workspace that supports creativity and teamwork.

By implementing the techniques discussed in this section, you can:
✅ Easily locate past whiteboards.
✅ Prevent clutter and disorganization.
✅ Ensure that important work is saved and accessible.

In the next section, we will explore Zoom Whiteboard's essential tools and features, including drawing tools, annotations, and media integrations.

2.2.3 Sharing Whiteboards with Others

One of the most powerful aspects of **Zoom Whiteboard** is its ability to facilitate seamless collaboration. Whether you're working with colleagues on a business strategy, brainstorming with a remote team, or teaching a virtual class, **sharing your whiteboard effectively** is crucial. This section will guide you through various ways to share your Zoom Whiteboard, adjust permissions, and collaborate efficiently.

---

1. Why Share a Zoom Whiteboard?

Before diving into the technical steps, it's important to understand **why sharing a Zoom Whiteboard is essential**:

- **Real-Time Collaboration** – Allows multiple users to contribute and edit in real time.

- **Enhanced Communication** – A visual aid helps teams organize thoughts and clarify ideas.

- **Seamless Accessibility** – Share whiteboards across different devices and Zoom platforms.

- **Efficient Brainstorming and Feedback** – Enables structured discussions, especially for remote teams.

- **Cross-Team and Cross-Department Integration** – Facilitates better teamwork across organizational boundaries.

Now, let's explore the different ways to **share a Zoom Whiteboard** and the best practices for doing so effectively.

2. Methods to Share a Zoom Whiteboard

There are multiple ways to share a **Zoom Whiteboard**, depending on your specific needs.

2.1 Sharing During a Zoom Meeting

When hosting a meeting, you might want to **share your whiteboard in real-time** so participants can contribute.

Steps to Share a Whiteboard in a Meeting:

1. **Open Zoom and Start a Meeting**

    o Launch Zoom and start or join a meeting.

2. **Access the Whiteboard**

    o Click **Share Screen** in the meeting toolbar.

    o Select **Whiteboard** from the options.

3. **Enable Editing for Participants**

- o By default, only the host can edit.

- o To allow collaboration, click **More** (three dots in the toolbar).

- o Select **Enable Annotation for Others**.

4. **Grant Specific Permissions**

- o You can allow everyone to edit or restrict editing to specific participants.

5. **End or Save the Whiteboard**

- o After the meeting, save your whiteboard for future reference.

 Pro Tip: Use the **"Spotlight" tool** to highlight key points while presenting your whiteboard.

2.2 Sharing a Whiteboard Outside a Meeting

You don't have to be in a live meeting to share a whiteboard. Zoom allows you to share and collaborate asynchronously.

Steps to Share a Whiteboard Outside a Meeting:

1. **Open Zoom Whiteboard**

- o Sign in to Zoom and go to the **Whiteboards** tab.

2. **Select the Whiteboard You Want to Share**

- o Click on a whiteboard from your saved list.

3. **Click the Share Button**

- o In the top-right corner, click the **Share** button.

4. **Choose Who Can Access It**

- o You can invite specific users by email or copy the link to share.

5. **Set Access Permissions**

- o Options include:

  - **Viewer:** Can only see the whiteboard.

- **Editor:** Can make changes and add content.
- **Owner:** Full control over the whiteboard.

6. **Send Invitations**

   o Click **Send** to notify participants via email or messaging apps.

Best Practice: If collaborating with external partners, **set an expiration date** for access to ensure security.

2.3 Sharing via a Link

For quick and easy access, you can share a **direct link** to your whiteboard.

How to Share a Whiteboard via Link:

1. Open the Whiteboard in Zoom
2. Click the "Share" Button
3. Copy the Generated Link
4. Choose Permission Settings (Viewer, Editor, or Owner)
5. Paste the Link in an Email, Chat, or Document

Tip: Use a **password-protected link** for added security.

2.4 Sharing with Zoom Chat or Email

You can send whiteboard access via Zoom's built-in chat feature or email.

Steps to Share via Zoom Chat:

1. Open Zoom Chat
2. Find the Contact or Group You Want to Share With
3. Click the Attach File Button and Select Whiteboard
4. Send the Whiteboard with a Custom Message

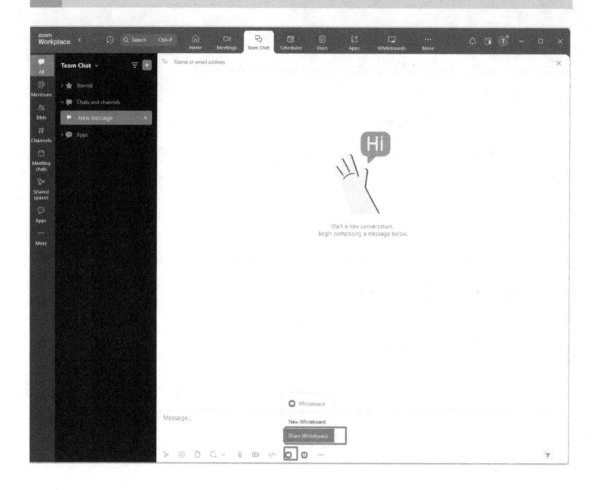

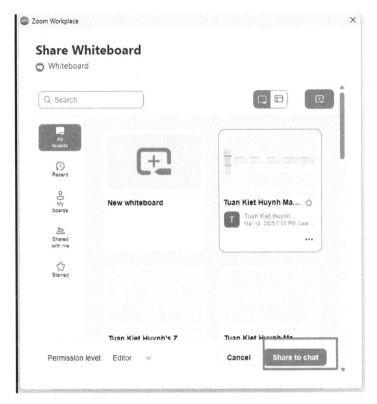

Alternatively, you can email an **access link** using Zoom's integration with Gmail or Outlook.

3. Managing Permissions and Access Levels

Controlling **who can edit or view your whiteboard** is critical for maintaining security and organization.

3.1 Understanding Permission Levels

Permission Level Description

Owner   Full access: edit, share, manage users, and delete whiteboard.

Editor   Can edit and add content but cannot delete or change ownership.

Viewer   Can only see the whiteboard but cannot make changes.

3.2 Adjusting Permissions

1. Go to Whiteboard Settings

2. Find the User You Want to Modify

3. Change Their Access Level

4. Click Save to Apply Changes

💡 **Tip:** Use **Editor mode** for trusted collaborators and **Viewer mode** for general audiences.

---

4. Best Practices for Sharing Whiteboards

To maximize collaboration and efficiency, follow these best practices:

Organize Your Whiteboards Properly

- Use folders for different projects.

- Name your whiteboards clearly (e.g., "Marketing Plan – Q1").

Control Access and Permissions Carefully

- Limit editing access to avoid accidental changes.

- Revoke access for inactive users after project completion.

Use Zoom Whiteboard Alongside Other Tools

- Integrate with Google Drive or Dropbox for easy file sharing.

- Use Slack or Microsoft Teams to notify team members about updates.

Regularly Save and Export Whiteboards

- Download as PDF or PNG for offline access.

- Save multiple versions to track progress.

---

5. Troubleshooting Common Issues

Even with a smooth workflow, **you may encounter issues** when sharing a Zoom Whiteboard.

Whiteboard Not Visible to Participants

- **Solution:** Check if you selected the right whiteboard when sharing.

Participants Cannot Edit the Whiteboard

- **Solution:** Go to settings and enable **Editor access**.

Link Sharing Not Working

- **Solution:** Ensure the link has the correct **permissions** enabled.

Whiteboard Disappeared After Meeting Ended

- **Solution:** Check the **Saved Whiteboards** section in Zoom.

---

6. Final Thoughts

Sharing a Zoom Whiteboard effectively enhances team collaboration, productivity, and engagement. By mastering the different sharing methods and best practices, you can seamlessly integrate whiteboarding into your workflow.

In the next chapter, we'll explore essential tools and features to help you unlock your creativity with Zoom Whiteboard.

2.3 Understanding the Zoom Whiteboard Interface

2.3.1 Toolbar Overview

The **Zoom Whiteboard toolbar** is the control center of the whiteboarding experience, providing users with a wide range of tools for drawing, annotating, collaborating, and organizing content. Understanding how to use these tools effectively is essential for maximizing productivity and creativity when using Zoom Whiteboard. This section will break down the toolbar into its key components, explaining each tool's purpose and functionality.

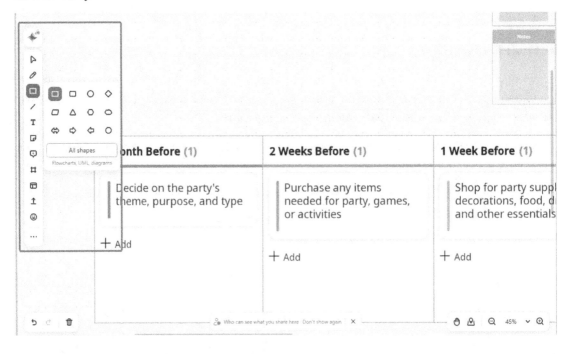

Overview of the Toolbar Layout

The toolbar in Zoom Whiteboard is typically located on the left-hand side of the screen in desktop versions and at the bottom for mobile devices. It consists of several key tools, each designed for a specific function, including **drawing, selecting, erasing, adding media, and collaboration features**.

Depending on the version of Zoom you are using, the toolbar may appear differently, but the core functionalities remain the same. Below is a breakdown of each tool and how to use it effectively.

Key Tools in the Zoom Whiteboard Toolbar

1. Selection Tool

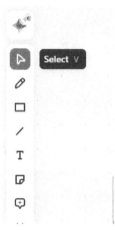

The selection tool (often represented by an arrow or hand icon) allows users to **select, move, resize, and rotate** objects on the whiteboard.

How to Use the Selection Tool:

- Click on an object to select it. A bounding box with resizing handles will appear.
- Drag the object to move it.
- Use the corner handles to resize the object proportionally.
- Rotate objects by clicking and dragging the rotation handle (if available).
- Hold **Shift** while resizing to maintain the object's proportions.

Best Practices:

- Use this tool to rearrange elements neatly on your whiteboard.
- Group multiple objects by holding **Shift** and clicking multiple items before moving them together.

- Utilize the alignment guides (if available) to organize objects efficiently.

2. Drawing and Annotation Tools

Zoom Whiteboard provides several drawing and annotation tools for freehand sketching and structured illustrations. These include the **pen, highlighter, and eraser**.

Pen Tool

- Used for freehand drawing and writing on the whiteboard.
- Supports different colors and line thickness adjustments.
- Ideal for sketching ideas, underlining important points, or handwriting notes.

Highlighter Tool

- Functions similarly to the pen but uses **transparent ink** to highlight text or objects.
- Available in multiple colors for organization and emphasis.
- Best used for emphasizing key points in shared discussions.

Eraser Tool

- Removes drawn lines and annotations without affecting shapes or text boxes.
- Click and drag over an area to erase specific portions.

- Some versions allow for **"clear all drawings"** if you want to remove everything quickly.

Best Practices:

- Use different colors for better organization of ideas.

- Keep lines and highlights clean for better readability.

- If working in a team, assign specific colors to different contributors for clarity.

3. Shape and Line Tools

For more structured diagrams and precise visuals, Zoom Whiteboard includes a set of **predefined shapes and lines**.

Available Shapes:

- **Rectangle, Circle, Triangle, and Polygon** – Used for diagrams, charts, and wireframes.

- **Arrows and Connectors** – Useful for flowcharts, mind maps, and directional indicators.

- **Lines and Curves** – Help in organizing content visually with separators.

How to Use Shapes:

- Click on the **Shape Tool** and select the desired shape.

- Click and drag on the canvas to create the shape.

- Use the formatting options to adjust **color, border thickness, and opacity**.

- Resize and rotate shapes using the selection tool.

Best Practices:

- Use **arrows** to indicate connections between ideas.

- Combine shapes with **text boxes** for easy-to-read diagrams.

- Maintain a **consistent size and alignment** for professional-looking layouts.

---

4. Sticky Notes and Text Boxes

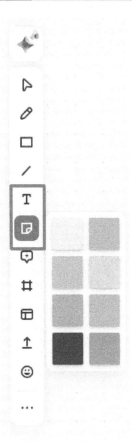

Sticky notes and text boxes are essential for adding structured content to the whiteboard.

Sticky Notes:

- Mimic physical sticky notes for brainstorming sessions.
- Available in multiple colors to categorize ideas.
- Can be **moved, resized, and grouped** as needed.

Text Boxes:

- Allow for longer text input compared to sticky notes.
- Support formatting options such as **bold, italic, underline, font size, and color**.
- Can be positioned anywhere on the whiteboard.

How to Use Them Effectively:

- Use **sticky notes** for quick thoughts and **text boxes** for more detailed explanations.

- Assign different colors for different topics or teams.

- Keep text brief and clear to ensure readability.

5. Insert Media (Images, PDFs, and Videos)

Zoom Whiteboard allows users to embed external media such as **images, PDFs, and videos** to enrich presentations and discussions.

Adding Images:

- Click on the **Insert Media Tool** and select **Image Upload**.

- Choose an image from your computer.

- Resize and move the image as needed.

Embedding PDFs:

- Upload multi-page PDFs for detailed reference materials.

- Navigate through pages within the whiteboard interface.

Inserting Videos:

- Paste a **YouTube or video link** (if supported) for quick playback.

- Ensure participants have access to external content.

Best Practices:

- Use images for **visual storytelling and infographics**.

- Upload PDFs for structured content like reports or case studies.

- Avoid cluttering the whiteboard with excessive media.

6. Collaboration and Sharing Tools

Zoom Whiteboard is designed for **real-time collaboration**, allowing multiple users to interact simultaneously.

Sharing and Permissions:

- Share whiteboards with specific individuals, teams, or public links.

- Adjust permissions: View, Comment, or Edit.

- Control access by enabling/disabling link sharing.

Commenting and Tagging:

- Use comments to provide feedback without altering the content.

- Tag teammates using **@mentions** for direct notifications.

Live Cursor Tracking:

- Enables visibility of each participant's cursor movements.

- Helps track contributions in real time.

Best Practices:

- Assign roles and responsibilities to prevent accidental edits.

- Use version history to track changes and revert if necessary.

- Establish clear communication guidelines when working in teams.

Conclusion: Mastering the Toolbar for a Seamless Experience

Understanding and effectively using the Zoom Whiteboard toolbar is the foundation for maximizing its potential. Whether you're brainstorming ideas, leading a business meeting, conducting a training session, or collaborating remotely, these tools empower you to create, organize, and share content effortlessly.

In the next section, we will explore advanced techniques and best practices for optimizing your workflow, using templates, and leveraging automation tools to enhance your whiteboarding experience.

2.3.2 Using Layers and Objects

Zoom Whiteboard provides a dynamic and flexible workspace that allows users to create, edit, and organize content efficiently. One of its most powerful features is the ability to work with **layers** and **objects**, which helps users manage complex whiteboards with multiple elements. Understanding how to use layers and objects effectively can significantly improve organization, collaboration, and workflow within Zoom Whiteboard.

In this section, we will explore the following:

- What are **layers** and **objects** in Zoom Whiteboard?

- How to **add, move, and organize objects**

- How to **work with layers** for better control

- Best practices for **using layers and objects efficiently**

1. Understanding Objects in Zoom Whiteboard

What Are Objects?

Objects refer to any individual element that you add to a Zoom Whiteboard, including:

- **Shapes** (circles, rectangles, arrows, etc.)

- **Lines and connectors**

- **Sticky notes and text boxes**

- **Images and embedded media**

- **Drawings and annotations**

Each of these objects can be independently manipulated, resized, and layered to create structured whiteboards. Objects are the **building blocks** of a whiteboard session, making it essential to understand how to work with them effectively.

Selecting and Moving Objects

To interact with objects on the whiteboard, follow these steps:

1. **Selecting Objects**:
   - Click on any object to select it.
   - Hold **Shift** to select multiple objects at once.

- o Use the **Lasso Tool** (if available) to select multiple objects by dragging around them.

2. **Moving Objects**:

   - o Click and drag the object to a new location.

   - o Use the **arrow keys** for precise positioning.

   - o Hold **Shift** while dragging to move the object along a straight path.

3. **Resizing and Rotating Objects**:

   - o Click on an object to reveal the **bounding box** with resizing handles.

   - o Drag the corners to resize the object proportionally.

   - o Rotate the object by selecting and dragging the **rotation handle** (usually a circular arrow).

4. **Copying and Duplicating Objects**:

   - o Use **Ctrl + C** (Windows) or **Cmd + C** (Mac) to copy.

   - o Use **Ctrl + V** (Windows) or **Cmd + V** (Mac) to paste.

   - o Right-click an object and select **Duplicate** to create a copy.

Grouping and Ungrouping Objects

Grouping objects allows users to manipulate multiple elements as a single unit, which is useful for organizing related content.

- **To Group Objects**:

1. Select multiple objects using **Shift + Click** or the **Lasso Tool**.

2. Right-click and choose **Group**.

3. The grouped objects can now be moved, resized, or rotated together.

- **To Ungroup Objects**:

    1. Select the grouped object.

    2. Right-click and choose **Ungroup**.

Grouping is particularly useful when creating flowcharts, diagrams, or structured layouts where multiple elements need to stay aligned.

---

2. Understanding Layers in Zoom Whiteboard

What Are Layers?

Layers in Zoom Whiteboard work like **transparent sheets stacked on top of each other**. They allow users to:

- Arrange objects in a **specific order** (e.g., bringing an object to the front or sending it to the back).

- Edit different parts of the whiteboard without affecting other elements.

- Create **structured and organized** content by keeping related objects together.

Layering Objects: Bring Forward and Send Backward

Each object on the whiteboard exists in a **layered structure**, meaning objects can be placed in front of or behind other objects.

- **Bring Forward / Bring to Front**

  o Moves an object **one step closer** to the front or brings it **to the very top layer**.

  o Right-click an object and choose **Bring Forward** or **Bring to Front**.

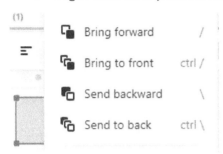

- **Send Backward / Send to Back**

  o Moves an object **one step behind** or **to the very bottom layer**.

  o Right-click an object and choose **Send Backward** or **Send to Back**.

Using Layers for Better Organization

1. **Creating Background Elements**:

   o Keep background shapes and templates in **lower layers** to avoid accidental edits.

   o Lock background elements by right-clicking and selecting **Lock Object**.

2. **Stacking Text and Annotations**:

   o Place text boxes **above** other elements so they remain visible.

   o Keep sticky notes on **higher layers** for emphasis.

3. **Working with Transparent Overlays**:

   o Use **semi-transparent shapes** on different layers to highlight sections.

   o Apply **color-coding** to differentiate layers visually.

3. Advanced Layering Techniques

Locking and Unlocking Layers

Locking a layer prevents accidental modifications while working on other elements.

- **Lock an Object or Layer**:
    - Right-click the object and choose **Lock Object**.
    - This prevents it from being moved or edited.
- **Unlock an Object or Layer**:
    - Right-click the locked object and choose **Unlock Object**.

This is especially useful when working with templates, guidelines, or background designs that should remain fixed.

Using Layers for Interactive Whiteboards

In collaborative sessions, layering can be used to:

- Separate teacher's notes from student contributions.
- Create interactive activities where elements appear in sequence.
- Develop multi-stage diagrams where users reveal content progressively.

For example, in a brainstorming session, the facilitator can:

1. Keep instructions on a locked background layer.
2. Allow participants to add sticky notes on a separate editable layer.
3. Organize contributions into categories on another layer.

Exporting and Saving Layered Whiteboards

When exporting a whiteboard, layers may be flattened into a single image or PDF. To preserve editing capabilities:

- Save the whiteboard within Zoom for future modifications.
- Export as a **Zoom-compatible file** for further editing.

4. Best Practices for Using Layers and Objects

To maximize efficiency while working with layers and objects:

✓ **Plan Your Whiteboard Layout**: Define sections before adding objects.

✓ **Use Consistent Layering**: Keep similar objects on the same layer.

✓ **Lock Background Elements**: Prevent accidental edits.

✓ **Group Related Objects**: Make it easier to move and edit content.

✓ **Organize Interactive Sessions**: Keep elements in layers for structured collaboration.

By mastering these tools, users can create well-structured, interactive, and visually appealing whiteboards that enhance communication and productivity.

Conclusion

Understanding **layers and objects** in Zoom Whiteboard is essential for efficient collaboration and content organization. By leveraging layering techniques, object manipulation, and grouping features, users can create professional and interactive whiteboards tailored to various needs—whether for business, education, or creative projects.

The next section will explore **Collaboration Features**, where we will learn how to invite participants, track changes, and use feedback tools effectively.

2.3.3 Navigating the Whiteboard Canvas

When using **Zoom Whiteboard**, understanding how to efficiently navigate the canvas is crucial for a smooth and productive experience. The whiteboard provides an **infinite canvas**, meaning you can expand your work area as needed, zoom in for detailed work, or zoom out to see the big picture. This section will guide you through various navigation techniques, including zooming, panning, and using shortcuts to move around the workspace efficiently.

1. Overview of the Whiteboard Canvas

The **Zoom Whiteboard Canvas** is designed to be flexible and easy to use, allowing you to create, organize, and collaborate without restrictions. Some of its key attributes include:

- **Infinite Canvas:** There are no predefined boundaries, meaning you can extend the whiteboard in any direction.

- **Fluid Navigation:** You can zoom in, zoom out, and move around effortlessly using different input methods (mouse, touchpad, touchscreen).

- **Scalable Elements:** Objects, drawings, and text adjust dynamically based on zoom levels, ensuring clarity at any scale.

- **Multi-User Friendly:** The whiteboard allows multiple users to navigate and interact simultaneously.

Before diving into navigation techniques, let's explore the **basic interface elements** that help you move around the canvas.

2. Navigation Methods

2.1 Using the Mouse or Trackpad

If you're using a desktop or laptop, the **mouse or trackpad** offers precise control over navigation. Here's how to move efficiently:

- **Zoom In and Out:**

    o Use the **scroll wheel** (mouse) or **pinch-to-zoom** (trackpad) to zoom in and out.

    o Alternatively, hold the **Ctrl (Windows) / Command (Mac) key** while scrolling for controlled zooming.

- **Panning Across the Canvas:**

    o Click and **drag with the right mouse button** to move around the whiteboard.

    o If using a trackpad, use **two fingers** to swipe in any direction.

- **Resetting the View:**

- Double-click on an empty space on the canvas to **center the view** back to its original position.

- Alternatively, use the **Fit to Screen** option from the toolbar.

2.2 Using Touch Controls (Tablet and Mobile Devices)

For those using Zoom Whiteboard on a **tablet or touchscreen device**, navigation is even more intuitive:

- Pinch-to-Zoom: Place two fingers on the screen and pinch in or out to zoom.

- Two-Finger Swipe: Use two fingers to pan in any direction.

- Tap and Hold: Long-pressing on an element allows you to reposition it smoothly.

- Double-Tap to Reset Zoom: This quickly brings the view back to the default scale.

2.3 Using Keyboard Shortcuts

Keyboard shortcuts can **speed up** navigation and improve workflow efficiency. Here are some essential shortcuts:

Action	Windows/Linux Shortcut	Mac Shortcut
Zoom In	Ctrl + +	Cmd + +
Zoom Out	Ctrl + -	Cmd + -
Fit to Screen	Ctrl + 0	Cmd + 0
Pan Left	Arrow Left	Arrow Left
Pan Right	Arrow Right	Arrow Right
Pan Up	Arrow Up	Arrow Up
Pan Down	Arrow Down	Arrow Down
Reset View	Ctrl + R	Cmd + R

Using these shortcuts can help you navigate without constantly reaching for the mouse, increasing productivity.

3. Zooming Strategies for Efficient Workflows

3.1 Working at Different Zoom Levels

- High-Level Overview: Zoom out (50%-75%) to see the full picture, useful for project planning and brainstorming.

- Detail Work: Zoom in (150%-200%) when working on specific sections or adding fine details.

- Split Workspaces: Use different zoom levels for different team members if collaborating.

3.2 Keeping Track of Your Location on the Canvas

- **Use the Mini-Map:**

  - Zoom Whiteboard provides a mini-map in some versions, allowing you to see an overview of your entire whiteboard.

  - This is especially helpful when working on large projects.

- **Mark Key Areas:**

  - Use colored backgrounds or section dividers to separate different parts of your whiteboard.

  - Label different areas with text boxes to make it easier to navigate later.

4. Managing Large Whiteboards

When dealing with large or complex whiteboards, keeping track of different elements is essential. Here are a few tips:

4.1 Structuring Your Whiteboard for Easy Navigation

- **Use Sections and Labels:**

  - Divide your canvas into sections using shapes or background colors.

  - Label sections clearly with text headers.

- **Create a Table of Contents:**

  - Use hyperlinks or sticky notes to create a navigation guide for easy access.

o   This is useful when presenting whiteboard content in a meeting.

4.2 Saving and Managing Views

- Use the "Fit to Screen" Button: Instantly resize everything to fit within your screen.

- Bookmark Key Areas: If Zoom introduces a bookmark feature, use it to quickly jump to frequently used sections.

- Save Multiple Versions: When working on long-term projects, periodically save different versions of your whiteboard.

5. Best Practices for Smooth Navigation

5.1 Avoid Clutter

A messy whiteboard can make navigation harder. To keep it clean:

- Regularly delete unused elements.

- Use color-coding and layers to organize content.

- Keep a consistent structure for different projects.

5.2 Train Your Team on Navigation Techniques

If working in a collaborative environment, ensure your team:

- Knows how to zoom, pan, and reset the view.

- Uses consistent shortcut keys.

- Organizes content in a structured manner.

6. Summary

Mastering Zoom Whiteboard navigation is essential for effective collaboration. By leveraging zooming techniques, keyboard shortcuts, and structured organization, you can create a seamless workflow and boost productivity. Whether you're brainstorming ideas, managing complex projects, or facilitating online meetings, smooth navigation ensures a stress-free experience.

Ready to explore more? In the next section, we'll dive into Essential Tools and Features to enhance your Zoom Whiteboard experience.

CHAPTER III
Essential Tools and Features

3.1 Drawing and Annotation Tools

3.1.1 Pen, Highlighter, and Eraser Tools

Zoom Whiteboard offers a variety of drawing and annotation tools that allow users to visualize ideas, highlight important details, and refine their work. Among these tools, the **Pen**, **Highlighter**, and **Eraser** are essential for sketching, annotating, and modifying content. Mastering these tools can enhance collaboration, making it easier to share thoughts and communicate effectively in virtual meetings and brainstorming sessions.

Understanding the Pen Tool

The **Pen Tool** in Zoom Whiteboard serves as the primary drawing instrument, allowing users to create freehand sketches, write notes, and illustrate concepts. It functions similarly to a real pen on paper but comes with additional customization options for enhanced digital drawing.

Features of the Pen Tool:

- Freehand Drawing – Enables users to draw anything from simple lines to complex shapes.

- Customizable Colors – Users can choose from a variety of colors to differentiate elements on the whiteboard.

- Adjustable Thickness – Different stroke widths are available to suit different needs, from fine lines to bold strokes.

- Smooth Handwriting – The pen tool supports handwriting, making it useful for taking quick notes or explaining concepts.

- Pressure Sensitivity (for stylus users) – When using a stylus, the pen tool can simulate real handwriting by adjusting line thickness based on pressure.

How to Use the Pen Tool in Zoom Whiteboard:

1. **Select the Pen Tool**

   o Open the Zoom Whiteboard.

   o Locate the toolbar at the bottom or side of the whiteboard interface.

   o Click on the **Pen Tool** icon.

2. **Customize the Pen Settings**

   o Click on the Color Palette to select a color.

   o Use the Stroke Thickness Slider to adjust the line thickness.

   o If using a stylus, check for pressure sensitivity options in settings.

3. **Start Drawing**

   o Click and drag your mouse or stylus across the whiteboard to draw.

   o Lift your pen (or release the mouse button) to finish a stroke.

4. **Modify Your Drawing**

   o If you make a mistake, use the **Eraser Tool** or **Undo Button** to remove unwanted strokes.

   o Use the **Selection Tool** to move or resize drawn elements.

Best Practices for Using the Pen Tool:

✓ Use different colors to categorize ideas (e.g., red for critical points, blue for supporting details).

✓ Choose an appropriate stroke thickness for better readability.

✓ Utilize handwriting recognition features if available.

✓ Avoid cluttering the whiteboard with excessive pen strokes.

Understanding the Highlighter Tool

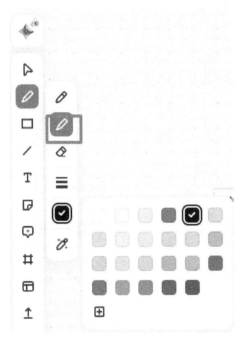

The Highlighter Tool is useful for emphasizing important sections of content, whether it be text, shapes, or handwritten notes. Unlike the pen, the highlighter applies a semi-transparent stroke, allowing users to mark information without obscuring it.

Features of the Highlighter Tool:

- **Semi-Transparent Overlay** – Allows highlighting over existing content without blocking visibility.

- **Multiple Colors** – Helps categorize different types of highlights (e.g., yellow for general importance, green for completed tasks).

- **Adjustable Thickness** – Users can select different highlighter widths to cover small or large areas.

How to Use the Highlighter Tool in Zoom Whiteboard:

1. **Select the Highlighter Tool**

    ○ Open the toolbar and click on the **Highlighter Icon.**

2. **Choose Your Color and Thickness**

    ○ Select a color from the palette.

    ○ Adjust the thickness to highlight specific words or entire sentences.

3. **Highlight Content**

    ○ Click and drag over text or objects to apply a highlight.

4. **Modify or Remove Highlights**

    ○ Use the **Eraser Tool** to remove unwanted highlights.

    ○ Change colors to reclassify highlights.

Best Practices for Using the Highlighter Tool:

✓ Use **yellow** for general emphasis, **green** for completed tasks, and **red** for urgent items.
✓ Avoid excessive highlighting—too many highlights can reduce readability.
✓ Use the **undo button** if you accidentally highlight the wrong section.

Understanding the Eraser Tool

The **Eraser Tool** allows users to remove unwanted annotations, making it easier to refine and adjust the whiteboard content. It is especially useful when making corrections or clearing space for new content.

Features of the Eraser Tool:

- **Precision Erasing** – Users can erase specific lines without affecting other elements.

- **Adjustable Eraser Size** – Provides flexibility in removing small details or large sections.

- **Clear All Option** – Quickly removes all drawings and annotations in one click.

How to Use the Eraser Tool in Zoom Whiteboard:

1. **Select the Eraser Tool**

   o Open the toolbar and click on the **Eraser Icon**.

2. **Choose Your Eraser Mode**

   o Use **small eraser** for detailed corrections.

   o Use **large eraser** to quickly clear large sections.

3. **Erase Content**

   o Click and drag over any pen strokes or highlights you want to remove.

4. **Use 'Clear All' (Optional)**

   o If you need to erase everything, select the **Clear All** button.

Best Practices for Using the Eraser Tool:

✓ Be careful when erasing—Zoom does not always offer an "undo" for large erasures.
✓ Use **small eraser mode** for minor corrections and **large mode** for clearing big sections.
✓ If you need to preserve work but make edits, consider using layers instead of erasing.

Conclusion

The **Pen, Highlighter, and Eraser Tools** in Zoom Whiteboard provide fundamental annotation capabilities that are essential for brainstorming, teaching, and remote collaboration. By mastering these tools, users can create more **engaging and organized** whiteboards, making meetings and presentations more effective.

In the next section, we will explore **3.1.2 Shapes and Lines**, where we discuss how to use predefined geometric elements to structure your whiteboard more efficiently.

3.1.2 Shapes and Lines

When working with **Zoom Whiteboard**, shapes and lines are essential tools for structuring ideas, creating diagrams, and enhancing collaboration. Whether you are designing a flowchart, mapping out a strategy, or simply emphasizing key points, understanding how to use shapes and lines effectively can significantly improve the clarity and organization of your whiteboard sessions.

This section will cover:

- The different types of shapes available in Zoom Whiteboard
- How to add, modify, and customize shapes
- Using lines for connections and organization
- Best practices for effective visual communication

---

1. Overview of Shapes in Zoom Whiteboard

1.1 Available Shape Options

Zoom Whiteboard provides a variety of **predefined shapes** that users can insert directly onto the canvas. These include:

- **Basic shapes:** Rectangle, Square, Circle, Oval
- **Polygons:** Triangle, Pentagon, Hexagon
- **Arrows:** Straight, Curved, and Double-Ended
- **Custom shapes:** Freehand drawing for unique visuals

Each of these shapes serves different purposes, from simple visual markers to complex flow diagrams.

1.2 Why Use Shapes?

Shapes are more than just decorative elements; they help organize and clarify information. Some key benefits include:

- Highlighting important points in a presentation
- Structuring diagrams for brainstorming or workflow mapping
- Grouping related ideas for better organization
- Enhancing readability by making content more visually appealing

For example, in **a team meeting**, a manager might use a **rectangle** to represent a project phase and an **arrow** to show dependencies between different tasks.

2. How to Add and Modify Shapes

2.1 Adding Shapes to the Whiteboard

To insert a shape in Zoom Whiteboard:

1. Open **Zoom Whiteboard** within a meeting or from the Zoom app.
2. Click on the **Shapes tool** in the toolbar.
3. Select the desired shape from the dropdown menu.
4. Click and drag on the whiteboard to draw the shape.

Once added, the shape remains interactive, meaning it can be resized, moved, or customized further.

2.2 Resizing and Moving Shapes

- **To resize a shape:** Click on the shape and drag any of its corner handles.

- **To move a shape:** Click and hold the shape, then drag it to a new location.

2.3 Customizing Shapes

Zoom Whiteboard allows users to customize shapes to match their design needs. Available customization options include:

- **Fill color:** Change the background color of the shape.

- **Border thickness:** Adjust the outline width for better visibility.

- **Opacity settings:** Make the shape transparent or solid.

- **Text labels:** Add text inside or next to a shape for explanation.

By customizing shapes, users can create **visually distinct elements** that improve clarity.

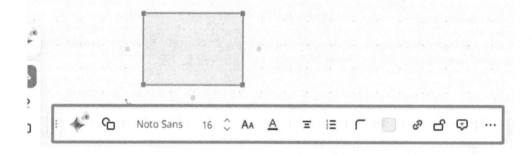

3. Using Lines for Connections and Organization

3.1 Types of Lines in Zoom Whiteboard

Lines are crucial for creating **connections** between different elements. Zoom Whiteboard provides multiple line options:

- **Straight lines:** Used for simple connections

- **Curved lines:** Useful for illustrating non-linear relationships

- **Arrows:** Indicate direction in workflows or processes

3.2 How to Draw and Edit Lines

To add a line to your whiteboard:

1. Select the **Line tool** from the toolbar.

2. Click and drag on the canvas to draw a straight or curved line.

3. Release the mouse to finalize placement.

Editing options include:

- Changing line thickness and color

- Adding arrowheads for directionality

- Connecting lines to shapes to create structured diagrams

3.3 Best Practices for Using Lines Effectively

- Maintain consistency by using the same line style across a diagram.

- Use arrows sparingly to avoid cluttering the whiteboard.

- Label connections when necessary for clarity.

For example, in **a business strategy session**, a facilitator might use lines to show **dependencies** between different action points.

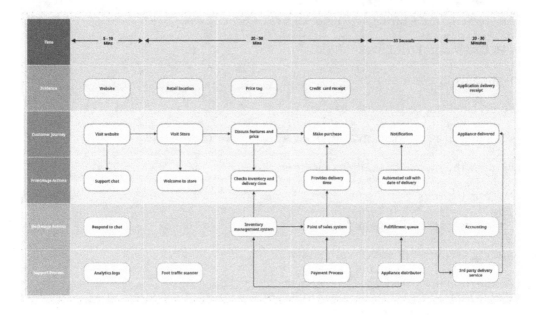

4. Practical Applications of Shapes and Lines

4.1 Business Use Cases

- Process Mapping: Use rectangles for tasks and arrows for transitions.

- Organizational Charts: Represent team structure with connected shapes.

- Brainstorming Sessions: Group ideas into different categories using color-coded shapes.

4.2 Educational Use Cases

- Mind Mapping: Use circles for core concepts and lines for related ideas.

- Visual Timelines: Show historical events using a combination of shapes and arrows.

- Mathematical Diagrams: Represent geometrical figures with predefined shapes.

4.3 Design and Creative Applications

- Wireframing UI/UX Designs: Use rectangles for interface elements.

- Storyboarding for Content Creation: Arrange visual scenes with connected shapes.

- Sketching Ideas Quickly: Use freehand drawing for early concepts.

5. Conclusion

Shapes and lines are fundamental tools in Zoom Whiteboard that enhance collaboration, clarity, and organization. By mastering these tools, users can create professional-looking whiteboards that improve communication and idea sharing.

In the next section, we will explore Adding Media and Interactive Elements, where you will learn how to incorporate images, videos, and external links into your whiteboards for an even richer experience.

3.1.3 Sticky Notes and Text Boxes

In Zoom Whiteboard, **Sticky Notes** and **Text Boxes** are essential tools that help users add textual content to their digital workspace. Whether you're brainstorming ideas, leaving feedback, or organizing information, these features provide a simple and effective way to communicate visually. This section explores how to use sticky notes and text boxes, their differences, customization options, and best practices for maximizing their effectiveness.

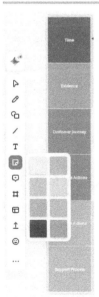

1. Introduction to Sticky Notes and Text Boxes

When working in a collaborative environment, visual clarity and structured communication are critical. Sticky notes and text boxes serve different but complementary functions:

- **Sticky Notes**: Designed for quick, colorful annotations, sticky notes help users jot down ideas, assign tasks, or add reminders. They mimic physical sticky notes, making them ideal for brainstorming sessions, agile workflows, and collaborative planning.

- **Text Boxes**: Unlike sticky notes, text boxes allow for more structured text input. They are typically used for longer descriptions, instructions, or formatted text content that requires more readability.

Both tools play a vital role in enhancing communication within Zoom Whiteboard, ensuring that information is visually organized and easy to follow.

2. How to Add and Use Sticky Notes

Adding sticky notes to your Zoom Whiteboard is straightforward. Follow these steps to get started:

2.1 Adding a Sticky Note

1. Open your **Zoom Whiteboard**.

2. Click on the **Sticky Note** icon from the toolbar (represented by a square or note symbol).

3. A new sticky note appears on the whiteboard. Click on it to start typing.

4. Press **Enter** to save your note.

2.2 Customizing Sticky Notes

Sticky notes in Zoom Whiteboard offer various customization options to improve visibility and organization:

- **Change Colors**: Select different colors to categorize notes (e.g., yellow for ideas, red for urgent tasks, green for approvals).

- **Resize and Move**: Click and drag the corners to adjust the size, or move the note anywhere on the board.

- **Duplicate Notes**: Right-click on a note and select **Duplicate** to create multiple copies quickly.

- **Tagging and Labeling**: Some versions of Zoom Whiteboard allow tagging notes with labels or assigning owners for task management.

- **Layering and Grouping**: Arrange notes in layers or group them together for better visual organization.

2.3 Collaborating with Sticky Notes

Sticky notes are highly effective in team collaboration. You can:

- Allow team members to add or edit notes in real time.

- Use **different colors for different teams or departments**.

- Organize sticky notes into sections based on workflow stages (e.g., "To-Do," "In Progress," "Completed").

💡 **Tip**: If you are conducting a brainstorming session, you can set a timer and ask participants to add their ideas using sticky notes, making it more interactive.

---

3. How to Add and Use Text Boxes

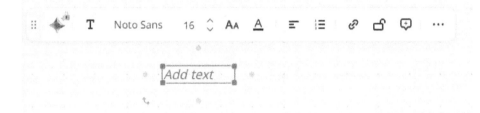

Text boxes provide more flexibility than sticky notes when adding structured content. They are ideal for instructions, explanations, and titles within the whiteboard.

3.1 Adding a Text Box

1. Open your **Zoom Whiteboard**.

2. Click on the **Text Box** tool from the toolbar (represented by a "T" icon).

3. Click anywhere on the board to create a text box.

4. Start typing to add content.

5. Press **Enter** to save.

3.2 Formatting and Customizing Text Boxes

Unlike sticky notes, text boxes offer advanced formatting options:

- Font Size and Style: Adjust font size, bold, italicize, or underline text.

- Background Color: Some text boxes allow background color changes for better emphasis.

- Alignment Options: Align text to the left, center, or right for better organization.

- Borders and Shadows: Add borders or shadow effects to highlight key information.
- Resizing and Positioning: Drag the edges to expand or shrink the text box.

3.3 Text Boxes for Organization and Presentation

Text boxes are widely used in structured whiteboard layouts:

- Headings and Titles: Use large text boxes for section headings.
- Instructions and Guidelines: Place explanatory text boxes near diagrams or sticky note clusters.
- Lists and Bullet Points: Use text boxes for structured content like lists or action plans.

💡 **Tip**: Combine text boxes with sticky notes to create Kanban boards, project plans, or workflow diagrams.

---

4. Best Practices for Using Sticky Notes and Text Boxes

To maximize efficiency when using sticky notes and text boxes, follow these best practices:

4.1 Keep It Clear and Concise

- Use short phrases on sticky notes for quick reference.
- For detailed explanations, use text boxes instead of multiple sticky notes.
- Avoid overcrowding—leave enough spacing for readability.

4.2 Use Colors Strategically

- Assign different colors for different categories.
- Use consistent color schemes (e.g., blue for discussions, green for approvals).
- Avoid excessive colors that create confusion.

4.3 Organize Notes for Better Workflow

- Use sticky notes for brainstorming, to-do lists, or feedback sessions.
- Use text boxes for instructions, titles, and structured content.

- Group sticky notes and text boxes into logical sections to create visual order.

4.4 Encourage Collaboration

- Assign ownership to sticky notes for task tracking.

- Allow team members to comment and edit on shared whiteboards.

- Periodically review and clean up outdated sticky notes and text boxes.

5. Real-World Applications of Sticky Notes and Text Boxes

Business Meetings and Team Collaboration

- Project Planning: Organize tasks into sticky note categories (To-Do, In Progress, Done).

- Meeting Notes: Summarize key points in text boxes for easy reference.

Education and Training

- Interactive Learning: Use sticky notes for Q&A, brainstorming, or topic discussions.

- Lesson Summaries: Use text boxes to outline key concepts.

UX and Design Workflows

- Wireframing: Use text boxes for labels and descriptions in prototypes.

- Feedback Collection: Sticky notes can represent user feedback in design sprints.

6. Conclusion

Sticky notes and text boxes are essential tools for improving collaboration and organization within Zoom Whiteboard. While sticky notes serve as quick visual markers for ideas and feedback, text boxes provide structured content for detailed communication. By using both strategically, teams can enhance productivity, improve workflow visualization, and make virtual collaboration more engaging.

By mastering these tools, you'll be able to create well-organized, visually appealing whiteboards that help your team work more efficiently and creatively.

💧 **Next Steps:** Try applying these techniques in your next Zoom Whiteboard session and see how they improve your workflow!

3.2 Adding Media and Interactive Elements

3.2.1 Inserting Images and PDFs

Zoom Whiteboard is not just a simple drawing tool—it is a powerful platform that allows users to incorporate multimedia elements such as **images and PDFs** to enhance presentations, brainstorming sessions, and collaborative projects. Adding visual components helps clarify complex ideas, improve engagement, and streamline workflows. This section will cover everything you need to know about inserting, managing, and optimizing images and PDFs in Zoom Whiteboard.

1. Why Use Images and PDFs in Zoom Whiteboard?

Visual elements play a crucial role in modern collaboration, especially in remote and hybrid work environments. Here's why integrating images and PDFs into your Zoom Whiteboard is beneficial:

- **Enhanced Communication** – A picture is worth a thousand words. Instead of lengthy explanations, a well-placed image can instantly convey an idea.

- **Improved Engagement** – Participants are more likely to stay focused and contribute when a whiteboard contains visual elements rather than just plain text.

- **Streamlined Workflows** – Uploading PDFs allows teams to review documents directly within the whiteboard, reducing the need to switch between applications.

- **Easier Conceptualization** – Diagrams, charts, and infographics help break down complex ideas into digestible visuals.

2. How to Insert Images into Zoom Whiteboard

2.1 Supported Image Formats

Zoom Whiteboard supports common image file types, including:

- **JPEG (.jpg, .jpeg)** – Best for standard images and photos.

- **PNG (.png)** – Supports transparent backgrounds, ideal for logos and icons.

- **GIF (.gif)** – Useful for simple animations or visual indicators.

- **SVG (.svg)** – Vector format for scalable graphics without losing quality.

2.2 Steps to Insert an Image

Method 1: Using the Toolbar

1. **Open Zoom Whiteboard** – Start a new whiteboard or open an existing one.

2. **Click the Upload Icon** – Look for the **"Upload"** button in the toolbar.

3. **Upload an Image** – Select an image from your computer or drag and drop it into the whiteboard.

4. **Resize and Position** – Adjust the size by dragging the corners of the image and move it to the desired location.

5. **Lock or Layer the Image** (Optional) – If needed, lock the image in place or position it behind other elements for layering effects.

Method 2: Copy-Paste from Other Sources

- Copy an image from your computer (Ctrl + C / Cmd + C) and paste it directly into the whiteboard (Ctrl + V / Cmd + V).

- Drag an image from a website or another application and drop it into the whiteboard.

2.3 Editing and Customizing Images

Once an image is inserted, you can modify it using Zoom Whiteboard's built-in tools:

- **Resize and Rotate** – Drag corners to resize or use the rotation handle to adjust orientation.

- **Transparency and Opacity** – Adjust the opacity for a watermark effect or better layering.

- **Cropping and Trimming** – Zoom Whiteboard may not have a built-in cropping tool, but you can pre-crop images before inserting them.

- **Annotations and Markups** – Use the drawing tools to add highlights, arrows, or notes over images.

3. How to Insert PDFs into Zoom Whiteboard

3.1 Why Use PDFs in Zoom Whiteboard?

PDFs are widely used for sharing structured documents, such as:

- Reports and business documents

- Lecture slides and training materials

- Reference guides and research papers

- Visual roadmaps and wireframes

3.2 Supported PDF Features in Zoom Whiteboard

When inserting a PDF into Zoom Whiteboard, you can:

- Upload multi-page PDFs

- Resize and move pages

- Annotate directly on top of the document

4. Best Practices for Using Images and PDFs in Zoom Whiteboard

Keep It Simple and Relevant

- Avoid overloading the whiteboard with too many visuals that may clutter the workspace.

- Use high-quality images that are easy to interpret.

Organize Your Content

- Use **layers** to position images behind or in front of other elements.

- Group related elements together for a structured layout.

Optimize for Performance

- Large image and PDF files may slow down Zoom Whiteboard. Compress files before uploading.

- Use vector graphics (SVGs) where possible for scalable visuals without losing quality.

5. Troubleshooting Common Issues

Image Not Uploading

- Ensure the file format is supported (JPEG, PNG, GIF, SVG).

- Check your internet connection.

- Reduce the file size if it exceeds Zoom's limits.

PDF Pages Not Displaying Correctly

- Convert complex PDFs to images before inserting.

- If annotations disappear, ensure the document is fully loaded before marking up.

6. Conclusion

Using **images and PDFs** in Zoom Whiteboard transforms it into a dynamic collaboration tool. Whether you're brainstorming, teaching, or planning, adding visual content makes information clearer, more engaging, and easier to understand. By mastering these features, you can maximize the potential of Zoom Whiteboard and enhance your digital workspace.

3.2.2 Embedding Links and Videos

Introduction

Incorporating external links and videos into a Zoom Whiteboard can significantly enhance collaboration and engagement. Whether you're embedding an instructional video, linking to a report, or providing quick access to an external resource, these features make your whiteboard more dynamic and informative. This section will walk you through the benefits, step-by-step instructions, and best practices for embedding links and videos in Zoom Whiteboard.

1. Why Embed Links and Videos in Zoom Whiteboard?

Enhancing Collaboration

Embedding links and videos allows teams to centralize their resources within a shared workspace. Instead of switching between multiple apps or screens, participants can access essential information directly within the whiteboard.

Improving Learning and Training

For educators and trainers, adding tutorial videos or external learning resources provides students with a more engaging experience. Video demonstrations can help explain complex concepts more effectively than static text or images.

Streamlining Workflows

Embedding links to documents, task management tools, or internal company portals can make workflows more efficient. For instance, project managers can link to task boards, while HR teams can embed company policies or onboarding materials.

Keeping Information Accessible

Instead of pasting long URLs in chat or emails, users can place hyperlinks directly within their whiteboards, making navigation easier for all participants.

2. How to Embed Links in Zoom Whiteboard

Adding a Hyperlink to a Whiteboard

Zoom Whiteboard allows users to insert hyperlinks that open external websites or resources. Here's how to do it:

1. **Open Zoom Whiteboard** – Ensure you are in an active whiteboard session.

2. **Select the Text Tool** – Click on the "Text" tool from the toolbar.

3. **Enter the Link Text** – Type the text that will serve as the clickable link (e.g., "Project Guidelines").

4. **Insert the Hyperlink** – Highlight the text, then look for the "Insert Link" option in the toolbar. Paste the desired URL.

5. **Save and Test** – Click outside the text box and hover over the link to test if it redirects properly.

Best Practices for Embedding Links

- **Use Descriptive Anchor Text** – Instead of pasting raw URLs, use meaningful text like "Company Handbook" or "Marketing Strategy 2024."

- **Ensure Accessibility** – Make sure all participants have permission to access the linked content.

- **Categorize Links** – If embedding multiple links, consider using a table or organizing them in sections for clarity.

---

3. How to Embed Videos in Zoom Whiteboard

3.1 Adding a Video from a URL (YouTube, Vimeo, etc.)

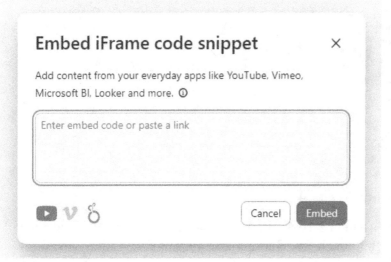

Zoom Whiteboard supports embedding videos from platforms like YouTube or Vimeo. Here's how to do it:

1. **Copy the Video URL** – Go to YouTube, Vimeo, or another supported platform and copy the video's shareable link.

2. **Open Zoom Whiteboard** – Make sure you are editing a whiteboard.

3. **Select the "Embed Video" Tool** – If available, click the "Insert Media" option.

4. **Paste the Video Link** – Zoom will automatically generate a video preview.

5. **Adjust Video Placement** – Resize or move the video frame as needed.

6. **Save and Play** – Click on the video to ensure it plays correctly within the whiteboard.

3.2 Uploading Videos Directly (If Supported by Zoom Whiteboard)

In some cases, Zoom may allow users to upload short video clips directly into the whiteboard. If this feature is enabled:

1. Select "Upload"

2. Choose a Video File from Your Device

3. Confirm Upload and Adjust Placement

3.3 Best Practices for Embedding Videos

- Keep Videos Short – For maximum engagement, use concise videos (1-5 minutes).

- Use High-Quality Content – Ensure videos are clear and relevant to your discussion.

- Provide Context – Include a short description next to the video explaining why it's included.

4. Use Cases for Embedded Links and Videos

Business Meetings and Team Collaboration

- Project Management – Link to Trello, Asana, or Jira task boards.

- Marketing Plans – Embed promotional videos to discuss strategies.

- Sales Presentations – Insert product demo videos for client pitches.

Education and Training

- Online Courses – Embed tutorial videos for students to watch.

- Interactive Lessons – Provide quick access to research articles or digital textbooks.

- Virtual Workshops – Link to pre-recorded training sessions.

Design and Creative Workflows

- UI/UX Design Reviews – Insert prototype videos for discussion.

- Content Creation – Link to brand guidelines or creative briefs.

- Brainstorming Sessions – Provide video inspiration for ideation.

5. Troubleshooting and Limitations

Common Issues and Fixes

Issue	Solution
Links Not Working	Ensure URLs are correctly formatted and accessible.
Video Not Playing	Check internet connectivity and video permissions.
Whiteboard Freezing	Refresh Zoom or restart the session.

Zoom Whiteboard Limitations

- Some platforms may not support embedded videos.

- Large video files may slow down whiteboard performance.

- External links may require additional authentication for restricted content.

6. Conclusion

Embedding links and videos in Zoom Whiteboard transforms a simple workspace into a powerful, interactive, and collaborative environment. Whether you are leading a business meeting, teaching an online class, or brainstorming a creative project, these features enhance communication and engagement. By following best practices, troubleshooting common issues, and maximizing use cases, you can leverage Zoom Whiteboard to its full potential.

Would you like to explore more advanced features in the next section? Let's dive deeper into the Collaboration Features of Zoom Whiteboard!

3.2.3 Using Smart Connectors

Introduction to Smart Connectors

Smart Connectors are one of the most powerful features of Zoom Whiteboard, enabling users to create dynamic and visually connected diagrams, mind maps, and workflows. Unlike traditional lines or arrows, Smart Connectors automatically adjust and adapt as you move elements around, maintaining the structure of your diagram. Whether you are mapping out processes, brainstorming ideas, or designing a flowchart, Smart Connectors help improve organization and clarity.

This section will guide you through everything you need to know about Smart Connectors, from basic functionality to advanced usage, ensuring you can maximize their potential in your Zoom Whiteboard sessions.

Understanding Smart Connectors

What Are Smart Connectors?

Smart Connectors are interactive lines or arrows that link objects on the whiteboard. They automatically reposition and maintain their connections when you move the linked objects, making it easier to manage complex diagrams without manually adjusting lines.

Key Features of Smart Connectors:

- *Automatic Adjustment*: When connected elements are moved, the connectors automatically reposition themselves.

- *Multiple Connection Points*: Objects can have multiple connectors linking them to other elements.

- *Customizable Styles:* Users can change the color, thickness, and style of the connectors to suit their visual needs.

- *Arrowheads and Line Styles*: Connectors can be customized with different types of arrowheads and line styles (solid, dashed, or dotted).

- *Supports Flowcharts and Diagrams*: Ideal for creating structured diagrams, such as organizational charts, process flows, and mind maps.

When to Use Smart Connectors

Smart Connectors are beneficial in many scenarios, including:

- *Process Mapping:* Illustrating workflows, step-by-step guides, or decision trees.

- *Brainstorming Sessions:* Connecting related ideas in a mind map.

- *Organizational Charts:* Showing hierarchical structures in a business or project.

- *Project Planning:* Visually linking tasks and dependencies in a planning session.

How to Use Smart Connectors in Zoom Whiteboard

Adding a Smart Connector

To add a Smart Connector in Zoom Whiteboard, follow these steps:

1. **Open the Whiteboard** – Navigate to your Zoom Whiteboard and select an existing board or create a new one.

2. **Select the Connector Tool** – Click on the **Smart Connector** icon from the toolbar (usually represented by a line or arrow symbol).

3. **Click on the First Object** – Hover over an object (e.g., a shape, text box, or sticky note). You will see anchor points where the connector can be attached.

4. **Drag to the Second Object** – Click and drag the connector to another object. The connector will snap into place, establishing a dynamic link between the two elements.

5. **Adjust the Connector as Needed** – If you move the connected objects, the Smart Connector will automatically reposition itself to maintain the connection.

Customizing Smart Connectors

Once you have added a Smart Connector, you can customize it using the following options:

- **Change Line Style:** Select the connector and choose between solid, dashed, or dotted lines.

- **Modify Arrowheads:** Add or remove arrowheads at either end of the connector.

- **Adjust Line Thickness and Color:** Customize the line thickness and color to match your diagram's theme.

- **Curve or Straighten Lines:** Adjust the curvature of the connector for better visual flow.

Managing Connectors in Complex Diagrams

When working with a large number of elements, it's important to keep connectors organized. Here are some best practices:

- **Use Grid Alignment:** Enable grid snapping to keep elements aligned properly.

- **Group Related Elements:** Use grouping tools to cluster related items together.

- **Color-Code Connections:** Assign different colors to connectors based on categories or relationships.

Advanced Uses of Smart Connectors

Creating Flowcharts and Process Diagrams

One of the most common applications of Smart Connectors is in building **flowcharts** and **process diagrams**. These are useful for:

- **Business workflows** (e.g., sales processes, customer support flows).

- **Decision trees** (e.g., if-then logic for troubleshooting).

- **Project planning** (e.g., task dependencies and Gantt chart representations).

Example: Building a Simple Flowchart

1. Add shapes (rectangles for processes, diamonds for decisions).

2. Use Smart Connectors to link each step logically.

3. Label the connectors with descriptions (e.g., "Yes" or "No" for decision branches).

4. Apply colors to different paths to distinguish between options.

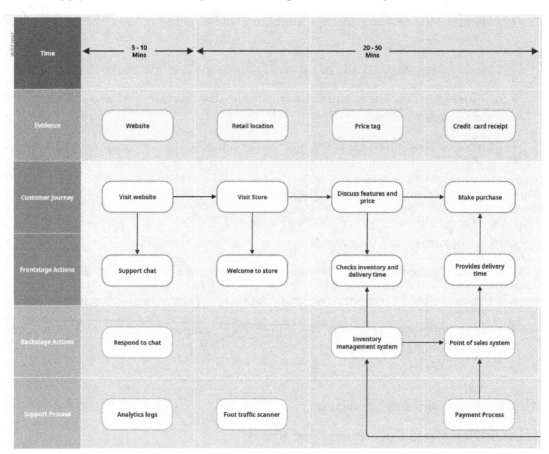

Using Smart Connectors for Mind Mapping

Smart Connectors are also ideal for **brainstorming sessions** and **mind maps**, allowing you to:

- Quickly branch out ideas from a central concept.
- Reorganize ideas dynamically without breaking connections.
- Use different styles of connectors to distinguish between categories.

Example: Creating a Mind Map

1. Start with a central topic (e.g., "Marketing Strategy").

2. Add subtopics (e.g., "Social Media," "SEO," "Email Campaigns").

3. Use Smart Connectors to visually link related concepts.

4. Adjust spacing and alignment to maintain clarity.

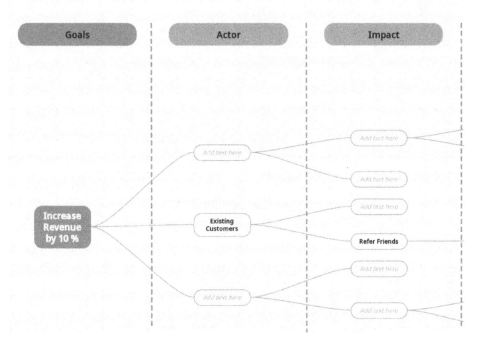

Integrating with External Tools

Zoom Whiteboard allows exporting diagrams with Smart Connectors to other applications, such as:

- PowerPoint – To use diagrams in presentations.

- Microsoft Visio or Lucidchart – For more advanced diagramming.

- Project Management Tools (Trello, Asana) – To translate visual workflows into actionable tasks.

Best Practices for Using Smart Connectors

To maximize the effectiveness of Smart Connectors, keep these best practices in mind:

1. Keep Diagrams Simple and Clear

- Avoid excessive connectors that make diagrams look cluttered.
- Use white space effectively to maintain readability.

2. Use Consistent Styles

- Maintain a uniform line style, thickness, and color scheme.
- Use different colors for different categories, but avoid too many variations.

3. Label Connectors When Necessary

- Add small text labels to clarify relationships between elements.
- Keep labels short and concise for quick understanding.

4. Regularly Save and Organize Whiteboards

- Use folders or categories to manage multiple whiteboards.
- Keep an archive of past versions for reference.

Conclusion

Smart Connectors in Zoom Whiteboard provide a powerful way to create structured, interactive, and dynamic diagrams for various purposes. Whether you're mapping out processes, brainstorming ideas, or planning projects, Smart Connectors simplify the way elements are linked, ensuring that your visuals remain organized and adaptable.

By mastering Smart Connectors, you can transform your Zoom Whiteboard into a collaborative and highly efficient workspace, helping you and your team communicate ideas more effectively and stay productive in virtual environments.

Next Steps

✓ **Practice creating different types of diagrams** using Smart Connectors.
✓ **Explore additional Zoom Whiteboard features** to enhance collaboration.
✓ **Experiment with exporting diagrams** to external tools for seamless integration.

3.3 Collaboration Features

3.3.1 Inviting Participants to Edit

Collaboration is at the heart of Zoom Whiteboard. The ability to invite participants to edit a whiteboard in real-time fosters teamwork, boosts productivity, and enhances brainstorming sessions. Whether you are working on a business strategy, an educational diagram, or a project plan, granting editing access allows multiple users to contribute their ideas seamlessly.

In this section, we will cover:

- The different levels of access for participants

- How to invite users to edit your whiteboard

- Managing and revoking editing permissions

- Best practices for effective collaboration

Understanding Access Levels in Zoom Whiteboard

Before inviting participants to edit a Zoom Whiteboard, it's essential to understand the different levels of access you can grant. Zoom offers multiple permission settings to ensure that collaboration remains secure and well-managed.

1. Viewer vs. Editor Permissions

When you share a whiteboard in Zoom, you can assign participants either **viewer** or **editor** permissions:

- **Viewer (Read-Only Access)** – Participants can see the content but cannot make changes. This is ideal for presentations, finalized plans, or when gathering feedback without allowing modifications.

- **Editor (Full Editing Access)** – Participants can modify the whiteboard, add elements, move objects, and delete content. This is useful for brainstorming sessions, collaborative design, or co-authoring documents.

2. Individual vs. Group Access

You can choose to invite:

- Specific individuals by adding their email addresses.

- All meeting participants when sharing in a live Zoom session.

- Users within your organization (if using Zoom Workplace for businesses).

- Public access with a shareable link (if enabled by your Zoom admin).

3. Temporary vs. Permanent Access

- **Temporary access** – Users can edit only during the meeting session. Once the meeting ends, their editing rights are removed.

- **Permanent access** – Participants can edit the whiteboard anytime, even outside of meetings. This is useful for long-term projects.

How to Invite Participants to Edit Your Whiteboard

1. Inviting Users During a Zoom Meeting

If you're using Zoom Whiteboard during a live meeting, inviting participants to edit is straightforward:

1. **Open the Whiteboard** – Click on the "Whiteboard" button in your Zoom meeting toolbar.

2. **Click "Share"** – In the top-right corner, find the "Share" button.

3. **Choose Participants** – Select from:
   - Everyone in the meeting (default option).
   - Specific individuals (enter their email addresses).
   - Organization members only (for enterprise accounts).

4. **Set Permissions** – Choose between **Viewer** or **Editor** access.

5. **Confirm and Share** – Click **Done**, and participants will receive a notification to join and edit the whiteboard.

💡 *Tip: If you want to maintain control, set participants as Viewers by default and only promote select users to Editors when necessary.*

2. Inviting Users Outside of a Meeting

You can also invite collaborators to edit a whiteboard outside of Zoom meetings, making it accessible anytime:

1. Go to the Zoom Web Portal or Desktop App.

2. Open Your Whiteboard Library.

3. Select the Whiteboard You Want to Share.

4. Click "Share" and Enter the Email Addresses of Participants.

5. Set Editing Permissions (Viewer or Editor).

6. Send Invitations.

Once invited, participants will receive an email or Zoom notification allowing them to access and edit the whiteboard.

Managing and Revoking Editing Permissions

To maintain control over your whiteboard, you might need to change or revoke editing permissions. Here's how:

1. Changing Participant Permissions

1. Open the Whiteboard.

2. Click on the "Share" button.

3. Locate the participant's name in the list.

4. Modify their access level:

   o Change from Editor to Viewer (if they no longer need to edit).

   o Change from Viewer to Editor (if they need to contribute).

5. Save Changes.

2. Removing Participants from the Whiteboard

If someone no longer needs access:

1. Open the Whiteboard Sharing Settings.

2. Find the user in the access list.

3. Click "Remove" next to their name.

4. Confirm the removal.

💡 *Tip: If you shared the whiteboard via a public link, you can disable the link to instantly revoke access for everyone who used it.*

Best Practices for Effective Collaboration

Now that you know how to invite and manage participants, let's explore some best practices to ensure smooth collaboration.

1. Set Clear Roles and Responsibilities

- Define who should edit the whiteboard and who should only view it.

- Assign different tasks to specific team members (e.g., one person handles diagrams, another takes notes).

2. Use Version History for Accountability

- Zoom Whiteboard allows you to track changes and restore previous versions if needed.

- Encourage team members to document major edits to maintain clarity.

3. Establish Collaboration Etiquette

- Avoid excessive overlapping of objects on the whiteboard.

- Use different colors or labels to distinguish individual contributions.

- Mute notifications if working asynchronously to avoid distractions.

4. Utilize Templates for Efficiency

- Instead of starting from scratch, use predefined templates for workflows, brainstorming, and project planning.

- Customize templates to fit your team's needs.

5. Keep Security in Mind

- Avoid sharing whiteboards publicly unless necessary.

- Regularly review access permissions and remove users who no longer need access.

Conclusion

Inviting participants to edit your Zoom Whiteboard unlocks powerful collaboration opportunities. By understanding access levels, managing permissions, and following best practices, you can enhance teamwork and streamline your workflow. Whether in live meetings or long-term projects, using Zoom Whiteboard effectively will elevate your virtual collaboration experience.

💡 *Next, we'll explore how to use Zoom Whiteboard's advanced features to maximize your productivity!*

3.3.2 Commenting and Feedback Tools

Collaboration is at the heart of Zoom Whiteboard, and the commenting and feedback tools play a crucial role in making teamwork efficient and seamless. Whether you are brainstorming ideas, reviewing project drafts, or teaching a class, the ability to provide real-time feedback enhances communication and improves outcomes. In this section, we will explore how to use comments and feedback tools effectively in Zoom Whiteboard to foster better collaboration.

1. Overview of Commenting and Feedback in Zoom Whiteboard

The **commenting and feedback system** in Zoom Whiteboard is designed to facilitate clear and structured discussions on ideas, diagrams, and content shared on the whiteboard. These tools enable users to:

- Leave comments on specific areas of the whiteboard.

- Reply to comments for threaded discussions.

- Tag users to direct feedback to specific collaborators.

- Resolve comments to mark feedback as addressed.

- Use emoji reactions to provide quick, informal responses.

These features help teams **streamline their communication** without the need for separate emails or chat messages, making collaboration more efficient.

---

2. Adding and Managing Comments in Zoom Whiteboard

2.1 How to Add Comments

Adding a comment in Zoom Whiteboard is simple and intuitive. Follow these steps:

1. **Select the Comment Tool**

   o Click on the **comment icon** (usually represented by a speech bubble) in the toolbar.

2. **Choose the Location**

   o Click anywhere on the whiteboard where you want to leave a comment.

   o If commenting on an object (e.g., text, image, shape), click directly on that element.

3. **Enter Your Comment**

   o A text box will appear where you can type your message.

   o You can format text (if supported) or use markdown-style shortcuts.

4. **Tag Specific Users (Optional)**

   o Use **@username** to notify specific collaborators.

   o Tagged users will receive a **notification** in Zoom.

5. **Post the Comment**

   o   Click **Submit** to add the comment to the whiteboard.

2.2 Editing and Deleting Comments

- **To edit a comment**, click on it and select the **edit option** (pencil icon).

- **To delete a comment**, click on it and select the **trash icon**.

- Deleted comments cannot be recovered, so use this option carefully.

3. Replying to and Resolving Comments

Replying to Comments

Zoom Whiteboard allows **threaded discussions**, making it easy to track conversations:

- Click on an existing comment.

- Type your response in the **reply box**.

- Press **Enter** to post the reply.

This is particularly useful in:

- **Team discussions**, where multiple people provide input.

- **Design reviews**, where changes need approval.

- **Education settings**, where teachers provide feedback to students.

Resolving Comments

Once feedback has been implemented, you can **resolve** comments:

- Click on the comment thread.

- Select the **"Mark as Resolved"** option.

- The comment will be hidden but can still be accessed in the **history**.

This feature keeps the whiteboard **clean** and ensures that only unresolved issues remain visible.

4. Using Emoji Reactions for Quick Feedback

For less formal feedback, **emoji reactions** allow users to respond **instantly** without leaving a detailed comment.

Adding an Emoji Reaction

- Click on an object, text, or comment.

- Choose the **emoji reaction** from the menu.

- The selected emoji appears as an overlay on the item.

When to Use Emoji Reactions

- 👍 **Thumbs up** – To approve an idea.

- 🎯 **Target** – To highlight a key point.

- 🚀 **Rocket** – To encourage innovation.

- 🛑 **Stop Sign** – To indicate an issue.

Emoji reactions work well for brainstorming sessions, feedback rounds, and quick approvals.

5. Best Practices for Using Comments and Feedback in Zoom Whiteboard

To ensure productive collaboration, follow these best practices:

Keep Comments Clear and Concise

- Avoid vague feedback like "This needs work." Instead, be specific:

  - ✓ *"This section is missing an example. Can you add one?"*

Use Mentions to Direct Feedback

- If feedback is intended for a particular person, tag them (@username) to ensure they see it.

Resolve Comments When Action is Taken

- Mark comments as resolved to maintain a clean workspace.

Set Commenting Guidelines for Teams

- Define rules for when to use comments vs. direct discussions.

Use Emojis for Quick Reactions

- Encourage team members to use emoji reactions for non-critical feedback.

6. Advanced Features and Future Enhancements

Zoom continuously updates its tools, and future enhancements may include:

- Voice comments – Allowing users to leave audio notes.

- AI-powered suggestions – Auto-generated feedback tips.

- Integration with project management tools – Syncing comments with Asana, Trello, or Jira.

Conclusion

The commenting and feedback tools in Zoom Whiteboard provide a powerful way to enhance collaboration. By using structured comments, replies, emoji reactions, and resolution tools, teams can work together more efficiently, ensuring clarity and productivity. Whether you are leading a brainstorming session, reviewing a project, or providing student feedback, mastering these tools will transform your virtual collaboration experience.

3.3.3 Version History and Recovery

Collaboration is at the heart of Zoom Whiteboard, enabling teams to work together seamlessly in real time. However, when multiple users contribute to a shared whiteboard, changes can sometimes be made unintentionally, important content may be deleted, or users may need to reference earlier versions of their work. This is where **Version History and Recovery** become essential.

Zoom Whiteboard provides a robust version history system that allows users to track modifications, restore previous versions, and maintain the integrity of their collaborative work. In this section, we'll explore how version history works, how to restore previous versions, and best practices for managing whiteboard revisions effectively.

Understanding Version History in Zoom Whiteboard

Version history in Zoom Whiteboard functions similarly to version tracking in other collaboration tools, like Google Docs or Microsoft OneDrive. It automatically saves snapshots of your whiteboard at different points in time, enabling users to view and restore previous versions when needed.

Key Features of Version History in Zoom Whiteboard

- **Automatic Saving:** Zoom Whiteboard periodically saves changes automatically, reducing the risk of data loss.

- **Time-Stamped Versions:** Each saved version is associated with a timestamp, showing when the changes were made.

- **Collaborator Attribution:** The system may track who made specific changes, allowing teams to identify contributors.

- **Multiple Restoration Points:** Users can access multiple historical versions, not just the most recent one.

This system ensures that no ideas or content are permanently lost, even in cases of accidental deletions or significant changes.

How to Access Version History in Zoom Whiteboard

Accessing version history in Zoom Whiteboard is simple and can be done by following these steps:

For Whiteboards in a Zoom Meeting:

1. Open the whiteboard you want to review.

2. Click on the **"More Options" (⋮)** button in the toolbar.

3. Select **"Version History"** from the dropdown menu.

4. A list of previously saved versions will appear, along with timestamps.

5. Click on any version to preview it.

For Whiteboards in Zoom Web Portal or Workplace App:

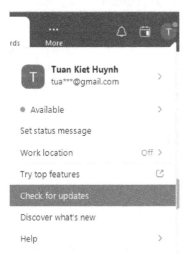

1. Log into your **Zoom Web Portal** or **Zoom Workplace App**.

2. Navigate to the **Whiteboards** section in the main menu.

3. Open the desired whiteboard.

4. Click the **Check for updates** button (usually found in the top-right menu).

5. Browse through previous versions and select one to restore if needed.

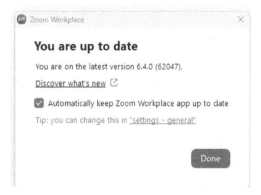

By following these steps, users can track modifications and retrieve older versions of their whiteboards effortlessly.

Best Practices for Managing Version History

To effectively use version history and recovery in Zoom Whiteboard, consider the following best practices:

1. Establish Naming Conventions for Versions

- If Zoom allows **manual saving with version names**, encourage users to add meaningful names to versions (e.g., "Project Plan – Initial Draft" or "Final Review Before Submission").

- Avoid vague version names like "Update 1" or "Test" to prevent confusion.

2. Regularly Review and Save Key Versions

- Periodically save significant changes as distinct versions so that you can revert to critical stages in the project.

- Before making substantial modifications, manually save the existing state as a checkpoint.

3. Assign Editing Permissions Wisely

- Limit full editing access to team leads or key collaborators.

- Use **view-only access** for stakeholders who need to review but should not alter the whiteboard.

- This prevents accidental deletions or unwanted modifications.

4. Train Your Team on Version Recovery

- Ensure all team members know how to access and restore versions.

- New users should receive guidance on undoing changes safely without disrupting workflow.

5. Keep Track of Who Made Changes

- If Zoom Whiteboard provides a collaborator history feature, review it regularly to identify who made specific modifications.

- This is especially useful for large teams working on a single whiteboard.

6. Use Version Control for External Collaboration

- When collaborating with external teams, create and maintain controlled versions before allowing edits.

- This ensures that external collaborators do not overwrite crucial internal discussions.

Limitations and Considerations

While version history in Zoom Whiteboard is powerful, it does have some limitations:

- **Storage Constraints:** Some versions may be auto-deleted after a certain period, depending on your Zoom plan.

- **Manual Saves:** Some versions might not be automatically saved if a user exits without syncing.

- **Collaborator Access:** Not all users may have permission to restore previous versions, depending on team settings.

💡 **Solution:** To mitigate these issues, always ensure auto-save is enabled, maintain manual backups of critical work, and adjust permission settings accordingly.

Future Enhancements and AI-Driven Versioning

Zoom is continuously evolving, and future updates may include:

- **AI-Powered Versioning:** AI might suggest the most relevant versions based on significant changes.

- **Advanced Comparison Tools:** Users could compare two versions side by side to identify differences.

- **Real-Time Change Tracking:** A more detailed change log that highlights each modification as it happens.

Keeping an eye on Zoom's updates will help users make the most of these upcoming improvements.

Conclusion

Version history and recovery in Zoom Whiteboard provide a safety net for collaborative work, ensuring that no idea is ever permanently lost. By understanding how to access, restore, and manage versions effectively, users can confidently experiment, refine, and improve their whiteboard content without the fear of making irreversible mistakes.

By applying best practices such as version naming, regular reviews, and permission management, teams can streamline their workflows and improve their efficiency when using Zoom Whiteboard.

The next chapter will dive deeper into **advanced techniques and best practices** for maximizing productivity with Zoom Whiteboard.

CHAPTER IV
Advanced Techniques and Best Practices

4.1 Organizing and Structuring Your Whiteboard

4.1.1 Using Layers and Grouping Elements

When working with Zoom Whiteboard, organizing elements efficiently can significantly improve clarity, collaboration, and overall usability. Using layers and grouping elements allows you to structure your content in a way that makes it easy to navigate, edit, and collaborate with others. This section will guide you through understanding layers, grouping elements, best practices for structuring content, and real-world use cases for these techniques.

Understanding Layers in Zoom Whiteboard

What Are Layers?

Layers in Zoom Whiteboard function similarly to layers in design software like Adobe Photoshop or Figma. They allow you to stack elements on top of each other and control their order, making it easier to organize content, hide certain elements, or emphasize key information.

For example, in a business planning session, you may want to have:

- A background layer with branding or guidelines.

- A content layer with text, shapes, and notes.

- A highlight layer that emphasizes key takeaways or action items.

Why Use Layers?

Using layers provides several advantages, including:

✓ **Better Organization** – Keeping related elements together improves clarity.

✓ **Easier Editing** – Move, hide, or adjust elements without disrupting other content.

✓ **Enhanced Collaboration** – Different team members can work on different layers.

✓ **Improved Focus** – Helps emphasize important points while keeping other details in the background.

How to Manage Layers in Zoom Whiteboard

Although Zoom Whiteboard does not have a traditional layer panel like Photoshop, you can manipulate elements in a layered fashion using the following techniques:

- Send to Back / Bring to Front – Right-click an object and move it forward or backward.

- Lock Background Elements – Prevent accidental changes by locking shapes or text.

- Use Transparent Elements – Overlay transparent shapes to create visual effects.

- Duplicate Key Layers – Copy a layer before making major changes to preserve earlier versions.

Grouping Elements for Better Organization

What Is Grouping?

Grouping elements allows you to combine multiple objects into a single unit, so you can move, resize, or edit them together. This is useful for structuring content efficiently, especially in complex whiteboards with many components.

For example:

- In a brainstorming session, you can group sticky notes related to the same topic.

- In a project plan, you can group tasks by priority or department.

- For a UI/UX wireframe, you can group sections of a website for easy adjustments.

How to Group and Ungroup Elements

1. **Select multiple elements** by holding down the **Shift key** while clicking each item.

2. Click on the **Group option** from the toolbar.

3. Now, moving one element will move the entire group.

4. To ungroup, select the group and click **Ungroup** from the menu.

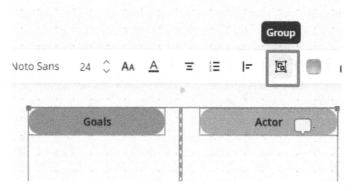

Benefits of Grouping Elements

✅ Faster Edits – Move and resize multiple elements at once.
✅ Consistent Formatting – Ensure uniform spacing and alignment.
✅ Easier Navigation – Keep related items together, reducing clutter.

Best Practices for Structuring Content with Layers and Groups

1. Maintain a Clear Hierarchy

Always structure your content in a way that prioritizes readability and navigation. Use different layers for:

- Background elements (company branding, general guidelines)

- Main content (diagrams, brainstorming notes, workflows)

- Highlight elements (key takeaways, action items, important dates)

2. Use Color Coding for Different Groups

Assign **specific colors** to different content types to improve visibility:
⬤ **Blue** – Ideas and brainstorming notes

☐ **Green** – Action items and tasks
☐ **Orange** – Warnings or blockers
● **Red** – Critical deadlines or issues

3. Lock Background Elements to Avoid Accidental Changes

If your whiteboard includes a reference diagram, grid, or framework, lock those elements in place so they do not accidentally move during collaboration.

4. Leverage Transparent Shapes for Layer Effects

If you need to highlight certain sections without covering them, use transparent colored shapes. This allows you to visually segment content without disrupting the overall view.

5. Organize Large Whiteboards into Sections

For whiteboards with a lot of content, divide them into logical sections:

📌 Top Left: Overview / Objectives
📌 Top Right: Key Topics / Ideas
📌 Bottom Left: Next Steps / Assignments
📌 Bottom Right: Additional Notes / References

This helps participants quickly locate information and prevents information overload.

Real-World Use Cases for Layers and Grouping

1. Business Strategy Meetings

A marketing team planning their next campaign can:

✓ Use background layers for branding and company guidelines.
✓ Use a content layer for brainstorming ideas and strategy.
✓ Use a highlight layer for key deadlines and priorities.

2. Remote Teaching and Learning

A teacher using Zoom Whiteboard for an online lesson can:

✓ Group lesson materials (text, images, diagrams) for easy movement.
✓ Layer interactive elements like quizzes and discussion prompts.
✓ Hide answers in a separate layer, revealing them when needed.

3. Project Management and Agile Workflows

A project manager conducting a Sprint planning session can:

✅ Use grouped sticky notes for task prioritization.

✅ Color-code teams for better workflow management.

✅ Lock completed tasks to prevent accidental changes.

Conclusion

Mastering layers and grouping elements in Zoom Whiteboard can drastically enhance the way you organize, present, and collaborate. Whether you're leading a business meeting, teaching a class, or brainstorming ideas, these techniques will streamline your workflow, improve clarity, and boost productivity.

Now that you understand how to structure your whiteboard, let's explore the next level of creativity in 4.1.2 Creating Templates for Reusability!

4.1.2 Creating Templates for Reusability

Templates are a powerful way to enhance efficiency and consistency when working with **Zoom Whiteboard**. By creating and using templates, you can streamline workflows, save time on repetitive tasks, and ensure that team members follow structured formats for brainstorming, planning, and collaboration. This section will guide you through the process of designing, saving, and utilizing reusable templates within **Zoom Whiteboard**.

---

1. Why Use Templates in Zoom Whiteboard?

Using templates can significantly improve workflow efficiency and collaboration. Here's why they matter:

Saving Time on Repetitive Tasks

Many teams frequently use whiteboards for similar purposes, such as project planning, team meetings, brainstorming sessions, and workflow diagrams. Instead of recreating the same structure every time, templates allow users to start with a predefined layout.

Maintaining Consistency Across Teams

Templates help standardize processes across an organization. Whether it's a weekly status meeting, a customer journey map, or a Kanban board, templates ensure that all team members follow the same structured format.

Reducing Setup Effort for New Users

For individuals who are new to Zoom Whiteboard, pre-built templates serve as a useful starting point. They can quickly understand the layout and contribute without needing to design a whiteboard from scratch.

2. Designing an Effective Whiteboard Template

Creating an effective template involves structuring content, choosing the right tools, and ensuring ease of use. Follow these steps to build a well-structured and reusable template.

2.1 Define the Purpose of Your Template

Before designing a template, ask yourself:

- What is the primary goal of this whiteboard?

- Who will be using it?

- How often will it be used?

For example, a Brainstorming Template might include predefined sections for ideas, feedback, and next steps, while a Project Planning Template may contain task lists, timelines, and responsible team members.

2.2 Choose the Right Layout and Structure

An effective template is visually organized and easy to navigate. Consider these best practices when structuring your template:

Use Clear Headings and Labels

- Divide your template into sections using **text boxes** or **sticky notes**.

- Label each area clearly (e.g., "Ideas", "Discussion Points", "Action Items").

Incorporate Color-Coding

- Use different colors to distinguish between categories or priorities.

- Example:

  - **Blue** for main topics

  - **Yellow** for brainstorming ideas

  - **Red** for urgent action items

Utilize Grid Layouts for Organization

- Align elements neatly using **grids** to create a structured appearance.

- Example: A **Kanban board** template should have well-defined columns such as **To Do, In Progress, and Completed**.

---

3. How to Create and Save a Template in Zoom Whiteboard

Once you've designed a structured whiteboard, you can save it as a reusable template. Follow these steps:

Creating the Template

1. Start a New Whiteboard: Open Zoom Whiteboard from your Zoom Web Portal or within a Zoom Meeting.

2. Add Essential Elements: Insert text, shapes, sticky notes, and images to define the structure.

3. Use Layers for Better Organization: If your template involves multiple sections, use layers to keep elements separate.

4. Test the Layout: Ensure that elements are properly aligned and that the template is easy to navigate.

Saving Your Template

1. Click the "Save" or "Export" Option: Zoom Whiteboard allows you to save whiteboards as files for future use.

2. Save as a Shared Template: If you are in a team workspace, store the template in a shared folder so others can access it.

3. Create a Naming Convention: Use clear names like "Project Kickoff Template" or "Brainstorming Session Template" to make templates easy to find.

4. Using Pre-Made Templates in Zoom Whiteboard

Accessing Built-In Templates

Zoom Whiteboard offers pre-made templates for various use cases. To use them:

1. Open a New Whiteboard

2. Select "Templates" from the Toolbar

3. Choose a Category (e.g., Brainstorming, Planning, Retrospective)

4. Customize the Template with your own content

Importing Custom Templates

If you've previously saved a whiteboard as a template, you can:

1. Go to Your Saved Whiteboards

2. Select the Template You Need

3. Duplicate It for New Use Cases

5. Best Practices for Managing Templates

Keep Templates Simple and Clean

- Avoid cluttered layouts—stick to essential elements only.

- Use icons and simple shapes instead of excessive text.

Update Templates Regularly

- If you frequently use a template, review it every few months to see if it needs improvements.

Ensure Templates Are Accessible

- Store templates in a shared team workspace so they are easily accessible.

- Set permissions so that team members can view or edit templates as needed.

6. Real-World Examples of Zoom Whiteboard Templates

Project Planning Template

- **Sections**: Task List, Responsible Team Members, Deadlines
- **Use Case**: Helps project managers keep track of deliverables

Brainstorming Template

- **Sections**: Ideas, Feedback, Next Steps
- **Use Case**: Encourages structured brainstorming sessions

Team Meeting Agenda Template

- **Sections**: Meeting Topics, Discussion Points, Action Items
- **Use Case**: Keeps virtual meetings focused and organized

7. Summary: Key Takeaways on Creating Templates

- Templates help save time, maintain consistency, and improve team collaboration.
- A well-designed template should have a clear structure, color coding, and easy navigation.
- You can create, save, and reuse templates in Zoom Whiteboard for different purposes.
- Using templates effectively ensures that teams can work more efficiently and collaborate seamlessly.

Next Steps

✓ Try creating a **custom template** in Zoom Whiteboard today!
✓ Explore built-in **Zoom templates** for inspiration.
✓ Share your **favorite templates** with your team for better collaboration.

4.1.3 Managing Large Whiteboards

As you become more proficient with Zoom Whiteboard, you may find yourself working on increasingly complex projects that require larger canvases, multiple layers of information, and numerous collaborators. Managing large whiteboards effectively ensures that your work remains organized, easy to navigate, and productive. This section will guide you through best practices for handling extensive whiteboard sessions, including structuring your content, optimizing performance, and enhancing collaboration.

1. Understanding the Challenges of Large Whiteboards

When working with large whiteboards, users often encounter several challenges:

- **Clutter and Information Overload** – As more content is added, the whiteboard can become difficult to navigate and interpret.

- **Navigation and Visibility Issues** – Scrolling through a large board can be time-consuming and may lead to lost ideas.

- **Collaboration Difficulties** – More collaborators mean more inputs, which can result in a chaotic working environment.

- **Performance Limitations** – Large whiteboards with extensive elements may cause lag or slow response times.

By addressing these challenges with the right techniques, you can maintain an efficient and structured workspace.

2. Structuring Your Whiteboard for Clarity

A well-structured whiteboard allows users to locate information quickly and enhances collaboration. Here's how you can organize your whiteboard effectively:

Use Sections and Zones

Dividing your whiteboard into sections or zones helps separate ideas and categorize content logically. Consider these approaches:

- Grid-Based Layout – Assign different areas for specific purposes (e.g., brainstorming, task planning, feedback).

- Color Coding – Use distinct colors for different sections or teams to make navigation easier.

- Labeling and Titles – Add clear titles and labels to help users understand each section's purpose.

Utilize Layers and Grouping Features

Zoom Whiteboard allows you to layer and group elements, making it easier to organize complex ideas.

- Create Layered Structures – Assign different topics to layers and toggle visibility when needed.

- Group Related Items – Select multiple objects and group them together to prevent accidental movement.

- Lock Important Sections – Lock key elements in place to maintain consistency in the layout.

Implement a Logical Flow

Designing a structured flow within your whiteboard makes it intuitive for viewers. Use:

- Directional Arrows – Guide users through the board using arrows or flowcharts.

- Numbered Steps – If your board follows a sequence, use numbered labels for clarity.

- Templates for Repeatable Workflows – Save templates for frequently used structures, reducing setup time.

3. Enhancing Navigation and Accessibility

A large whiteboard is only useful if users can navigate it efficiently. Here are ways to improve accessibility:

Zoom and Pan Controls

Train your team on using zoom and pan features effectively:

- Use Keyboard Shortcuts – Familiarize yourself with shortcuts for zooming in and out quickly.

- Enable Mini-Map or Overview Mode – If available, activate a mini-map to see the entire board at a glance.

- Strategic Placement of Key Content – Keep frequently referenced content near the center for easy access.

Link Key Sections with Navigation Shortcuts

For whiteboards with multiple sections, hyperlinks or navigation buttons can improve movement between areas:

- Create Clickable Elements – Insert links that jump to specific whiteboard sections.

- Anchor Points – Use reference markers to direct users to relevant areas.

- Interactive Menus – Design a floating menu with quick-access links to important sections.

Search and Tagging System

For boards with massive amounts of content, search and tagging features help users locate information quickly:

- Assign Tags to Elements – Categorize sticky notes, text, or images with specific keywords.

- Use Search Functionality – If supported, leverage search tools to find key terms or topics.

- Create an Index Section – Dedicate an area to list important items with reference numbers.

4. Optimizing Performance and Preventing Lag

As a whiteboard grows, performance issues may arise. Here's how to optimize it for smooth operation:

Reduce Excessive Elements

- Limit High-Resolution Images – Large images slow down responsiveness; use compressed versions instead.

- Delete Unnecessary Objects – Periodically clean up old or unused elements.

- Avoid Excessive Animations – If using animations or transitions, ensure they don't overload the system.

Break Large Whiteboards into Multiple Boards

For extremely complex projects, consider:

- Creating Multiple Linked Boards – Instead of one massive board, divide content across smaller boards with navigation links.

- Using Sections as Independent Workspaces – Assign different teams their own whiteboard areas.

- Archiving Older Versions – Save past iterations separately to reduce the current board's size.

Adjusting Device and Network Settings

To maintain smooth whiteboard performance:

- Use a High-Speed Internet Connection – Lag often results from poor connectivity.

- Optimize Device Settings – Ensure your computer or tablet meets Zoom's recommended specifications.

- Update Zoom Regularly – Keep software up to date for performance enhancements.

5. Managing Collaboration on Large Whiteboards

As more people contribute to a whiteboard, maintaining order becomes crucial. Here's how to manage large teams effectively:

Set Clear Editing Permissions

- Restrict Access for Certain Users – Assign view-only roles for non-editors.

- Enable Moderator Controls – Designate facilitators to organize input.

- Use Revision History – Track changes and revert if needed.

Establish Guidelines for Contributions

To maintain clarity in large group collaborations:

- Define a Contribution Protocol – Decide who adds content and where.

- Encourage Naming Conventions – Have users label their contributions for easy identification.

- Schedule Regular Cleanup Sessions – Dedicate time to organizing and decluttering the board.

Utilize Comments and Feedback Tools

Instead of cluttering the board with additional notes:

- Use the Comment Feature – Keep discussions in the comments rather than on the board itself.

- Assign Tasks Within the Whiteboard – If possible, tag users for specific actions.

- Archive Completed Sections – Move resolved discussions to a separate area to free up space.

6. Final Thoughts: Mastering Large Whiteboards

Handling large Zoom Whiteboards efficiently requires a combination of organization, navigation strategies, performance optimizations, and structured collaboration techniques. By implementing the best practices outlined in this section, you can:

✔ Keep content structured and easy to follow

✔ Improve navigation for all users

✔ Optimize performance for smoother operation

✔ Facilitate effective collaboration on extensive whiteboards

As you work with increasingly complex whiteboards, continue experimenting with different layouts, workflows, and automation features to streamline your process. By doing so, you can unlock the full potential of Zoom Whiteboard, making it a powerful tool for brainstorming, planning, and teamwork.

4.2 Interactive Brainstorming and Mind Mapping

4.2.1 Setting Up a Brainstorming Session

Brainstorming is a powerful technique used in problem-solving, innovation, and collaboration. With Zoom Whiteboard, teams can conduct brainstorming sessions in a dynamic and visually engaging way, regardless of their location. This section will guide you through the best practices, step-by-step setup, and advanced techniques to make your brainstorming sessions effective using Zoom Whiteboard.

1. Understanding the Purpose of Brainstorming with Zoom Whiteboard

Before setting up a brainstorming session, it's important to define its purpose. Whether you are solving a problem, generating creative ideas, or planning a project, having a clear objective will help structure the session efficiently.

Why Use Zoom Whiteboard for Brainstorming?

- Real-time collaboration – Multiple users can contribute simultaneously.

- Visual representation – Ideas can be categorized, linked, and modified with ease.

- Templates and tools – Built-in tools help structure brainstorming sessions effectively.

- Remote-friendly – Team members can participate from anywhere, making it ideal for distributed teams.

2. Preparing for the Brainstorming Session

A well-organized brainstorming session requires **proper preparation**. Follow these key steps:

Define the Session Goals

Clearly articulate what you want to achieve. Some common objectives include:

- Generating new product ideas

- Solving a business challenge

- Improving an internal process

- Planning a marketing campaign

Select the Right Participants

A brainstorming session should include diverse perspectives to maximize creativity. Consider inviting:

- Team members from different departments

- Subject matter experts

- Stakeholders or end-users

Choose the Right Zoom Whiteboard Template

Zoom Whiteboard offers pre-made templates for brainstorming, such as:

- Mind Maps – Ideal for exploring interconnected ideas.

- SWOT Analysis – For strategic decision-making.

- Affinity Diagrams – Useful for grouping and categorizing ideas.

- Flowcharts – Helps visualize processes and workflows.

If no template fits your needs, you can create a custom whiteboard layout before the meeting.

Set Up Collaboration Rules

To keep the session productive:

- Encourage free-thinking and judgment-free idea sharing.

- Use a time limit for idea generation.

- Assign a facilitator to keep discussions on track.

3. Setting Up a Brainstorming Session in Zoom Whiteboard

Opening and Preparing the Whiteboard

1. Start a Zoom Meeting – Open Zoom and create a new meeting or join an existing one.

2. Access Zoom Whiteboard – Click on the "Whiteboard" option in the toolbar.

3. Create a New Whiteboard – Select "New Whiteboard" and choose a blank canvas or a template.

4. Enable Collaboration – Click on the "Share" button to allow participants to edit.

Structuring the Whiteboard for Brainstorming

Use the following structure to ensure a smooth brainstorming flow:

1. Central Idea – Place the main topic in the center using a Text Box or Shape Tool.

2. Idea Branches – Create branches for different categories using lines or arrows.

3. Idea Contribution – Encourage participants to add sticky notes, drawings, or images.

4. Voting and Refining – Use emoji reactions or color coding to prioritize ideas.

💡 *Pro Tip:* Assign different colors to different participants for easy identification.

4. Running an Effective Brainstorming Session

Icebreaker Activity

Begin with a quick warm-up exercise to encourage creative thinking. Example activities:

- Random Word Association – Generate ideas based on a random word.

- Worst Idea Exercise – List bad ideas first to lower creative barriers.

Encouraging Participation

- Turn on Video & Audio – This makes the session more interactive.

- Use the Chat Feature – Allows quieter participants to contribute.

- Time-Limited Rounds – Give participants 5-10 minutes per brainstorming round.

Categorizing and Refining Ideas

Once ideas are listed, group them into categories:

- Use Affinity Diagrams to organize related concepts.

- Use Mind Mapping to connect ideas logically.

- Highlight or color-code high-priority suggestions.

💡 *Pro Tip:* Use the "Comment" feature in Zoom Whiteboard to discuss specific ideas.

5. Concluding the Brainstorming Session

Summarizing the Discussion

- Review the top ideas visually on the whiteboard.

- Use the "Export to PDF" feature to save the session for later reference.

Assigning Action Items

- Identify next steps based on selected ideas.

- Assign owners to different tasks.

- Set a follow-up meeting to review progress.

Sharing the Whiteboard

- Click "Share" to distribute the brainstorming results via email, Slack, or Google Drive.

6. Advanced Techniques for Brainstorming with Zoom Whiteboard

Integrating AI and Automation

Zoom Whiteboard includes AI-powered features such as:

- AI Idea Suggestions – Helps generate additional creative insights.

- Smart Formatting – Automatically aligns elements for clarity.

Using Zoom Whiteboard with Other Tools

- Google Docs & Notion – Document key findings.

- Trello & Asana – Convert ideas into actionable tasks.

- Miro & MURAL – Export whiteboards for further refinement.

Improving Virtual Brainstorming Culture

- Establish brainstorming norms within your team.

- Rotate facilitators to encourage different styles.

- Regularly experiment with new brainstorming techniques.

7. Final Thoughts

A well-structured brainstorming session on Zoom Whiteboard fosters creativity, teamwork, and problem-solving. By following these steps and best practices, you can maximize idea generation and collaboration, leading to innovative solutions in your team or organization.

✅ **Key Takeaways:**

- Define clear goals and select the right participants.

- Use **templates and structured layouts** to streamline brainstorming.

- Encourage **active participation** and refine ideas effectively.

- Integrate **AI tools and third-party apps** for better productivity.

- Save and share the whiteboard to ensure follow-up actions.

By mastering **Zoom Whiteboard brainstorming**, you can unlock **your team's full creative potential** and drive innovation from anywhere!

4.2.2 Using Mind Maps for Idea Generation

Introduction to Mind Mapping in Zoom Whiteboard

Mind mapping is a powerful visual thinking tool that helps individuals and teams brainstorm, organize ideas, and develop strategies in a structured yet flexible way. With Zoom Whiteboard, users can create digital mind maps that facilitate collaboration and enhance creativity. Whether you are planning a project, structuring a presentation, or solving complex problems, mind maps can make your thought process clearer and more effective.

In this section, we will explore how to use mind maps for idea generation in Zoom Whiteboard, including step-by-step instructions, best practices, and real-world applications.

Understanding the Basics of Mind Mapping

What is a Mind Map?

A mind map is a diagram that visually organizes information around a central idea or concept. It starts with a central node and expands outward with branches that represent related ideas, topics, or tasks. These branches can further expand into sub-branches, creating a hierarchical structure that captures relationships between different elements.

Benefits of Using Mind Maps in Zoom Whiteboard

- Enhanced Creativity – Encourages free thinking and idea expansion.

- Better Organization – Structures thoughts logically, making complex ideas easier to understand.

- Improved Collaboration – Allows teams to contribute ideas in real time.

- Efficient Problem-Solving – Helps break down challenges into manageable parts.

- Memory and Retention – The visual structure makes information easier to recall.

Creating a Mind Map in Zoom Whiteboard

Step 1: Setting Up the Central Idea

1. Open Zoom Whiteboard and create a new board.

2. Select the Text Tool and type the main idea in the center of the board.

3. Use Shapes or Sticky Notes to visually distinguish the central idea.

4. Adjust the size and color to make it stand out.

Step 2: Adding Main Branches

1. Identify the key topics related to your central idea.

2. Use Lines or Smart Connectors to create branches extending from the center.

3. Label each branch with a relevant keyword or concept.

4. Use different colors for each branch to improve readability.

Step 3: Expanding with Sub-Branches

1. For each main branch, add sub-branches to explore related details.

2. Use additional lines or arrows to connect ideas logically.

3. Group similar concepts together to maintain structure.

4. Consider using icons or symbols for visual emphasis.

Step 4: Enhancing the Mind Map with Media

1. Add images, screenshots, or diagrams to support ideas.

2. Embed links to relevant documents or websites for further reference.

3. Use sticky notes for additional explanations or reminders.

Step 5: Refining and Organizing the Mind Map

1. Rearrange elements for better clarity and flow.

2. Resize and reposition items to avoid clutter.

3. Ensure branches are evenly spaced for easy readability.

4. Save the mind map for future collaboration and updates.

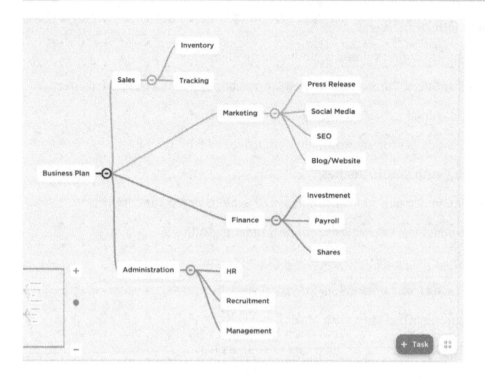

Best Practices for Effective Mind Mapping

Keep it Simple and Clear

- Use short phrases or single words instead of long sentences.
- Maintain a clean and uncluttered layout.
- Limit the number of branches to avoid complexity.

Use Colors and Visual Cues

- Assign different colors to branches for categorization.
- Use icons and symbols to highlight important points.
- Utilize bold or italic text to differentiate key ideas.

Encourage Collaboration

- Allow team members to add ideas in real time.

- Use Zoom's commenting feature for feedback.

- Assign specific colors or sections to different contributors.

Integrate with Other Zoom Tools

- Link the mind map to Zoom Meetings for live discussions.

- Export the mind map as an image or PDF for sharing.

- Use Zoom recording and transcription to document brainstorming sessions.

Real-World Applications of Mind Maps in Zoom Whiteboard

1. Brainstorming New Business Strategies

Companies use mind maps to explore growth opportunities, develop marketing plans, and refine business models.

2. Structuring Educational Content

Teachers and trainers organize lesson plans, course structures, and key learning points using mind maps.

3. Managing Projects and Tasks

Project managers break down tasks, set deadlines, and visualize dependencies through structured mind maps.

4. Developing Creative Content

Writers, designers, and content creators outline ideas, map storylines, and plan creative projects using mind maps.

5. Problem-Solving and Decision-Making

Teams analyze complex issues, explore solutions, and make informed decisions by visually mapping out options.

Conclusion

Mind mapping in Zoom Whiteboard is a versatile and effective tool for idea generation, planning, and collaboration. By following best practices and leveraging Zoom's features, individuals and teams can enhance their creativity, improve organization, and drive innovation. Whether you are brainstorming for business, education, or creative work, a well-structured mind map can transform your workflow and decision-making process.

◆ **Next Steps:**

- Try creating your first mind map in Zoom Whiteboard.

- Explore advanced features like **AI-assisted mind mapping** and **third-party integrations**.

- Share your mind map with your team and collect feedback for improvement.

4.2.3 Connecting Ideas with Flowcharts

In the world of brainstorming and mind mapping, flowcharts serve as a powerful tool for structuring and connecting ideas logically. Zoom Whiteboard provides a flexible and user-friendly platform to create and manipulate flowcharts in real-time, making it easier for teams to visualize complex ideas, workflows, and processes.

This section will guide you through the importance of flowcharts in brainstorming, the core elements of an effective flowchart, and how to create, edit, and optimize flowcharts using Zoom Whiteboard.

1. Why Use Flowcharts for Idea Connection?

Flowcharts are particularly useful for:

- Structuring ideas logically – Instead of listing disconnected thoughts, flowcharts establish clear relationships between concepts.

- Breaking down complex ideas – A large project or problem can be simplified into smaller, manageable steps.

- Enhancing team collaboration – Teams can work together to build a shared understanding of processes, workflows, and solutions.

- Providing a visual representation of thought processes – Seeing how ideas connect fosters better decision-making.

Common Scenarios for Using Flowcharts in Zoom Whiteboard

- Problem-solving sessions – Teams can map out causes, solutions, and decision paths.

- Project planning – Structuring tasks in a logical sequence.

- Business workflows – Visualizing approval processes, operations, and task delegation.

- Education and training – Helping students understand cause-and-effect relationships.

2. Core Components of a Flowchart

Before creating a flowchart in **Zoom Whiteboard**, it's important to understand the basic elements used in flowchart design:

Flowchart Symbols and Their Functions

- Start/End (Terminator Symbol) – Represented by an oval, this marks the beginning or end of a process.

- Process (Rectangle) – Indicates an action or task that needs to be performed.

- Decision (Diamond) – Represents a decision point, often leading to different outcomes based on a yes/no or true/false choice.

- Arrow (Connector) – Shows the flow of the process, connecting different elements logically.

- Input/Output (Parallelogram) – Represents an input action (e.g., entering data) or an output result (e.g., displaying information).

Understanding these basic symbols ensures that your flowcharts are structured in a clear, universally recognizable format.

Creating Flowcharts in Zoom Whiteboard

Zoom Whiteboard provides multiple tools to create flowcharts easily. Follow these steps to create an effective, interactive flowchart:

Step-by-Step Guide to Creating a Flowchart

Step 1: Open Zoom Whiteboard and Select a Blank Canvas

- Access Zoom Whiteboard through the Zoom app or web portal.

- Start a new whiteboard and ensure you have editing permissions.

Step 2: Use Shapes to Represent Steps

- Select the shapes tool from the toolbar.

- Drag and drop the Start/End (Oval) shape to mark the beginning of the process.

- Add Rectangles (Processes), Diamonds (Decisions), and Parallelograms (Input/Output) as needed.

Step 3: Connect Shapes with Arrows

- Use the arrow tool to link different shapes.

- Adjust the arrows to show clear, logical progression.

- Use smart connectors to ensure flexibility when moving elements.

Step 4: Label Each Step Clearly

- Double-click on each shape to add text labels.

- Keep labels short and descriptive for easy understanding.

Step 5: Apply Colors and Formatting

- Color-code different elements to highlight decision points or specific steps.

- Use bold or underlined text for important stages.

Step 6: Test the Flowchart

- Walk through the process to ensure logical consistency.

- Make adjustments to optimize clarity and effectiveness.

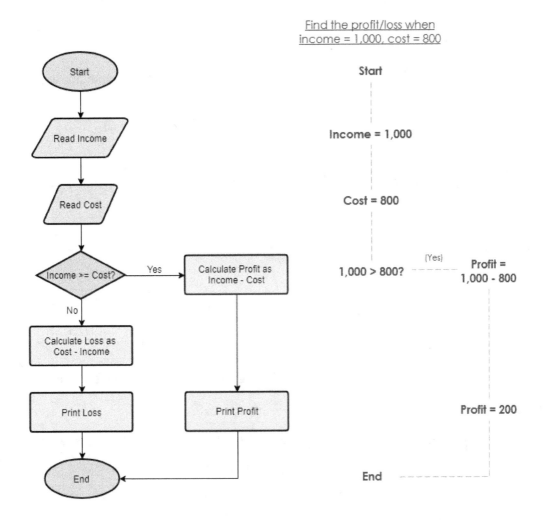

4. Optimizing Flowcharts for Collaboration

Best Practices for an Effective Flowchart

1. Keep it simple – Avoid excessive details that can overwhelm viewers.

2. Use clear labeling – Each step should have a concise and meaningful title.

3. Ensure logical flow – Every process should lead smoothly into the next step.

4. Make it interactive – Utilize Zoom Whiteboard's real-time collaboration features for team input.

5. Regularly update and refine – As ideas evolve, adjust the flowchart accordingly.

Collaborative Features to Enhance Flowcharting in Zoom Whiteboard

- Real-Time Editing – Team members can add, modify, and comment on the flowchart in real time.

- Sticky Notes and Annotations – Used for feedback and suggestions.

- Version History – Allows tracking of changes and refinements.

- Exporting and Sharing – Easily share the flowchart as a PDF or image for reference.

5. Real-World Applications of Flowcharts in Zoom Whiteboard

Business Applications

- Decision-making frameworks – Mapping out possible choices and consequences.

- Customer journey mapping – Understanding how customers interact with a product or service.

- Employee onboarding processes – Visualizing steps for new hire integration.

Educational Use Cases

- Lesson planning – Structuring educational modules for better student engagement.

- Concept explanation – Breaking down complex subjects into clear steps.

- Student projects – Helping students organize research ideas effectively.

Project and Task Management

- Task delegation – Assigning responsibilities visually within a team.

- Event planning – Structuring timelines and responsibilities.

- Product development – Mapping out the design and launch phases.

6. Conclusion: Enhancing Creativity and Productivity with Flowcharts

Flowcharts are an indispensable tool for organizing thoughts, mapping out processes, and making better decisions. Zoom Whiteboard's intuitive features make it easy to create, edit, and collaborate on flowcharts in real time.

By mastering flowcharting techniques, you can:

✓ Improve team collaboration and brainstorming sessions.
✓ Streamline complex processes into clear visual workflows.
✓ Make better decisions based on well-structured frameworks.

Incorporate flowcharts into your daily work to unlock greater productivity, creativity, and efficiency with Zoom Whiteboard!

Next Steps:

◆ Try creating a simple flowchart using Zoom Whiteboard.
◆ Experiment with smart connectors and decision points.
◆ Use color coding to improve clarity.
◆ Explore Zoom Whiteboard's advanced collaboration tools.

By implementing these strategies, you'll transform your brainstorming and workflow visualization skills using Zoom Whiteboard like a pro!

4.3 Maximizing Productivity with Zoom Whiteboard

4.3.1 Keyboard Shortcuts and Quick Actions

Introduction

Efficiency is key when using any digital collaboration tool, and Zoom Whiteboard is no exception. Mastering keyboard shortcuts and quick actions can significantly enhance your productivity, allowing you to navigate the interface seamlessly, create content faster, and streamline collaboration. This section explores essential shortcuts, time-saving techniques, and best practices to maximize efficiency with Zoom Whiteboard.

Why Use Keyboard Shortcuts?

Keyboard shortcuts reduce the time spent clicking through menus, making tasks quicker and more intuitive. Whether you are drawing, adding text, organizing elements, or navigating your whiteboard, shortcuts enhance workflow speed and accuracy. Some key benefits include:

- Increased speed: Perform tasks with fewer clicks.

- Improved accuracy: Reduce the chance of selecting incorrect tools.

- Better multitasking: Quickly switch between tools while brainstorming.

- Enhanced accessibility: Users with mobility impairments can work more efficiently.

Essential Zoom Whiteboard Keyboard Shortcuts

Below is a list of the most important keyboard shortcuts for Zoom Whiteboard. These will help you work faster and maintain a smooth creative flow.

1. Navigation Shortcuts

These shortcuts help you move around your whiteboard quickly:

- Pan across the whiteboard → Space + Drag Mouse

- Zoom in → Ctrl + Scroll Up (Windows) / Command + Scroll Up (Mac)

- Zoom out → Ctrl + Scroll Down (Windows) / Command + Scroll Down (Mac)

- Fit to screen → Ctrl + 0 (Windows) / Command + 0 (Mac)

- Jump to the previous section → Shift + Left Arrow

- Jump to the next section → Shift + Right Arrow

2. Drawing and Annotation Shortcuts

When working on diagrams, mind maps, or brainstorming ideas, these shortcuts will make the process smoother:

- Select Pen Tool → P

- Select Highlighter Tool → H

- Select Eraser Tool → E

- Undo last action → Ctrl + Z (Windows) / Command + Z (Mac)

- Redo last action → Ctrl + Y (Windows) / Command + Shift + Z (Mac)

- Change line thickness → Ctrl + [+] or [-]

- Change line color → C (Opens color picker)

3. Text and Shape Shortcuts

Quickly add and edit text or shapes with these shortcuts:

- Insert Text Box → T

- Bold text → Ctrl + B (Windows) / Command + B (Mac)

- Italicize text → Ctrl + I (Windows) / Command + I (Mac)

- Underline text → Ctrl + U (Windows) / Command + U (Mac)

- Align text left → Ctrl + L

- Align text center → Ctrl + E

- Align text right → Ctrl + R

- Insert Rectangle → R

- Insert Circle → O

- Insert Line → L

- Group selected elements → Ctrl + G (Windows) / Command + G (Mac)

- Ungroup selected elements → Ctrl + Shift + G (Windows) / Command + Shift + G (Mac)

4. Object and Element Manipulation Shortcuts

To arrange objects efficiently on your whiteboard, use these:

- Move selected object → Arrow Keys

- Duplicate selected object → Ctrl + D (Windows) / Command + D (Mac)

- Delete selected object → Delete or Backspace

- Bring object forward → Ctrl +] (Windows) / Command +] (Mac)

- Send object backward → Ctrl + [(Windows) / Command + [(Mac)

- Lock an object in place → Ctrl + L

- Unlock an object → Ctrl + Shift + L

5. Quick Collaboration Shortcuts

When working with others, these shortcuts streamline communication:

- Open Chat Panel → Ctrl + Shift + C

- Mute/Unmute Microphone → M

- Start/Stop Screen Sharing → Ctrl + Shift + S (Windows) / Command + Shift + S (Mac)

- Invite Participants → Ctrl + I (Windows) / Command + I (Mac)

Using Quick Actions for Faster Workflow

Besides keyboard shortcuts, quick actions in Zoom Whiteboard help users perform frequent tasks with minimal effort. These actions allow you to automate repetitive processes and improve efficiency.

1. Quick Access Toolbar

- Customize the Quick Access Toolbar for frequently used tools like pen, text, and shape tools.

- Right-click on any tool and select "Add to Quick Toolbar" for faster selection.

2. Right-Click Menus for Contextual Actions

- Right-click on any object to access quick formatting, duplication, or deletion options.

- Use "Align" and "Distribute" options for perfectly structured layouts.

3. Using Templates for Quick Setups

- Save frequently used layouts as templates to avoid rebuilding them from scratch.

- Access pre-made templates from Zoom Whiteboard's library for brainstorming, project planning, and workflows.

4. Auto-Align and Smart Guides

- Enable Smart Guides to automatically align objects when moving them.

- Zoom Whiteboard offers grid snapping to keep elements perfectly positioned.

Best Practices for Mastering Keyboard Shortcuts and Quick Actions

1. Memorize the most-used shortcuts: Start with basic navigation and drawing tools, then expand to text and object manipulation.

2. Create a cheat sheet: Keep a printed or digital list of shortcuts until they become second nature.

3. Practice with real tasks: Apply shortcuts during actual brainstorming sessions, team meetings, or solo projects.

4. Customize your quick access tools: Prioritize frequently used features to minimize distractions.

5. Use shortcuts across different devices: Zoom Whiteboard works on desktop, tablets, and mobile devices, so practice across platforms.

Conclusion

Using keyboard shortcuts and quick actions in Zoom Whiteboard significantly enhances productivity and workflow efficiency. By integrating these time-saving techniques, users can spend more time creating and collaborating rather than navigating menus. Whether you are brainstorming ideas, managing projects, or teaching students, these shortcuts help you make the most of Zoom Whiteboard's capabilities.

Next Steps

To continue improving your efficiency:

- Practice the shortcuts daily until they become second nature.

- Explore additional automation tools within Zoom Workplace.

- Combine shortcuts with other productivity techniques like templates and structured layouts.

By mastering these techniques, you'll be able to unlock the full potential of Zoom Whiteboard and boost your creative collaboration!

4.3.2 Automation and AI-Assisted Features

As digital collaboration tools continue to evolve, automation and artificial intelligence (AI) are playing an increasingly important role in improving efficiency and streamlining workflows. Zoom Whiteboard has integrated various AI-assisted features and automation tools that help users save time, organize content more effectively, and enhance creativity.

In this section, we will explore how automation and AI-assisted features in Zoom Whiteboard can boost your productivity, including:

- AI-powered formatting and layout adjustments

- Smart object recognition and auto-grouping

- Automatic template suggestions

- Speech-to-text and handwriting recognition

- Integration with third-party automation tools

1. AI-Powered Formatting and Layout Adjustments

One of the most useful automation features in Zoom Whiteboard is AI-assisted formatting and layout adjustments. These features help users organize their ideas more effectively without spending too much time manually adjusting elements.

1.1 Auto-Align and Smart Layouts

When working with a large whiteboard, manually aligning objects such as text boxes, shapes, and images can be time-consuming. Zoom Whiteboard provides an auto-align feature that automatically arranges elements in a clean and structured way.

How it works:

- When you add multiple elements to the whiteboard, Zoom detects patterns and suggests optimal layouts.

- You can enable "Smart Layout" to automatically distribute objects evenly, ensuring a professional and polished appearance.

- Clicking the "Auto-Align" button instantly tidies up misaligned content.

Best Use Cases:

- Organizing brainstorming sessions with many sticky notes.

- Structuring flowcharts and diagrams efficiently.

- Creating mind maps without worrying about alignment.

1.2 Intelligent Resizing and Scaling

Another AI-assisted feature in Zoom Whiteboard is intelligent resizing, which ensures that elements remain proportionally adjusted when you resize them.

Key benefits:

- Automatically resizes grouped elements while maintaining aspect ratios.

- Prevents distorted shapes when enlarging or shrinking content.

- Allows for zooming in and out without losing clarity.

2. Smart Object Recognition and Auto-Grouping

Zoom Whiteboard includes smart object recognition, which automatically detects and categorizes different elements such as shapes, text, and images. This feature helps streamline organization and enhances collaboration.

2.1 AI-Based Shape Recognition

When drawing shapes manually, Zoom Whiteboard AI automatically converts rough sketches into perfect circles, squares, triangles, and arrows.

How to use:

- Draw a rough circle or rectangle on the whiteboard.

- Zoom automatically snaps it into a perfect geometric shape.

- This feature works with arrows, lines, and custom polygons as well.

Best Use Cases:

- Quickly sketching flowcharts and process diagrams.

- Drawing UX wireframes for design and prototyping.

- Enhancing visual clarity in live meetings.

2.2 Auto-Grouping for Related Content

AI can also detect related objects and suggest grouping them together. This prevents clutter and allows for better organization.

Example:

- If you place multiple sticky notes on a whiteboard, Zoom can recognize related notes and group them into clusters based on keywords.

- You can use one-click grouping to automatically organize items, saving time during brainstorming sessions.

3. Automatic Template Suggestions

Another powerful automation feature in Zoom Whiteboard is its ability to recommend templates based on the content of your session.

3.1 AI-Powered Template Selection

When you start a new whiteboard, Zoom can analyze your keywords and objects and suggest relevant templates such as:

- Kanban Boards (for project management)
- Flowcharts (for process visualization)
- Mind Maps (for brainstorming)
- SWOT Analysis (for strategic planning)

How it helps:

- Saves time by providing structured formats.
- Ensures consistency in meeting workflows.
- Helps new users get started without having to manually design layouts.

4. Speech-to-Text and Handwriting Recognition

AI-powered speech-to-text and handwriting recognition are game-changing features for those who want to capture ideas quickly and effortlessly.

4.1 Speech-to-Text for Instant Note-Taking

Zoom Whiteboard includes a built-in speech-to-text converter that allows users to speak their ideas instead of typing them.

How to use:

1. Enable voice input from the Zoom Whiteboard toolbar.
2. Speak naturally, and AI will transcribe your words into text.
3. The text is automatically formatted into sticky notes or text boxes.

Best Use Cases:

- Taking quick meeting notes without typing.
- Transcribing brainstorming sessions in real-time.
- Enabling accessibility for users with disabilities.

4.2 Handwriting Recognition for Digital Notes

If you prefer writing with a stylus or touchscreen, Zoom Whiteboard can convert your handwriting into editable text.

How it works:

- Write using a stylus or your finger.

- AI automatically recognizes and converts handwritten words into text.

- The converted text can be formatted, resized, and moved like any other element.

Best Use Cases:

- Digital note-taking during online classes.

- Creating annotated documents for team projects.

- Quickly sketching ideas and converting them into formal notes.

5. Integration with Third-Party Automation Tools

Zoom Whiteboard also supports integration with automation platforms such as Zapier, Microsoft Power Automate, and Google Workspace, allowing users to create custom workflows.

5.1 Automating Whiteboard Workflows

With third-party automation tools, you can:

- Automatically save whiteboards to Google Drive or OneDrive.

- Trigger notifications in Slack or Microsoft Teams when a whiteboard is updated.

- Export Zoom Whiteboard content directly into Asana, Trello, or Monday.com for project tracking.

5.2 AI-Enhanced Meeting Summaries

After a meeting, Zoom's AI can:

- Generate a summary of whiteboard discussions.

- Extract action items and next steps.

- Send an automated follow-up email to all participants.

Best Use Cases:

- Streamlining project management tasks.

- Ensuring meeting action items are well-documented.

- Reducing the need for manual note-taking.

Conclusion

Automation and AI-assisted features in Zoom Whiteboard significantly enhance efficiency, organization, and creativity. From smart layouts and automatic grouping to speech-to-text and third-party integrations, these tools streamline collaboration and help users focus on ideas instead of manual adjustments.

By leveraging these powerful AI tools, you can maximize productivity, improve teamwork, and create professional-looking whiteboards with minimal effort. Whether you're using Zoom Whiteboard for business, education, or creative projects, embracing automation will elevate your workflow and enhance the digital collaboration experience.

4.3.3 Integrating with Other Zoom and Third-Party Tools

Zoom Whiteboard is a powerful collaboration tool on its own, but its true potential is unlocked when integrated with other Zoom features and third-party applications. By connecting Zoom Whiteboard with additional tools, users can streamline workflows, enhance productivity, and create a more efficient virtual workspace.

This section explores how Zoom Whiteboard integrates with other Zoom services, productivity applications, and external platforms to optimize collaboration. We will cover:

- Integrating Zoom Whiteboard with Other Zoom Features

- Connecting Zoom Whiteboard with Productivity and Cloud Storage Tools

- Using APIs and Automation to Extend Zoom Whiteboard Capabilities

Integrating Zoom Whiteboard with Other Zoom Features

Zoom offers a suite of tools designed to enhance communication and collaboration. Integrating Zoom Whiteboard with these features can improve meeting efficiency and team productivity.

A. Zoom Meetings and Zoom Whiteboard

One of the most natural integrations is between **Zoom Meetings** and **Zoom Whiteboard**. Participants can use the whiteboard to brainstorm, take notes, or create visual representations of ideas in real time.

Key Benefits:

- Share and edit a whiteboard during a Zoom meeting.

- Allow multiple participants to collaborate in real time.

- Save whiteboard sessions for future reference and follow-ups.

How to Enable Zoom Whiteboard in Meetings:

1. Start or join a Zoom meeting.

2. Click on the Whiteboard option in the meeting toolbar.

3. Select New Whiteboard or choose an existing whiteboard.

4. Share the whiteboard with participants and begin collaborating.

B. Zoom Rooms and Whiteboard Collaboration

For businesses using **Zoom Rooms**, the integration of Zoom Whiteboard allows teams to collaborate in hybrid environments where in-office and remote team members can contribute equally.

Best Practices for Zoom Rooms and Whiteboard:

- Use large touchscreen displays for interactive brainstorming.

- Enable persistent whiteboards so teams can continue working asynchronously.

- Use breakout rooms for small group collaborations, then bring ideas back to the main whiteboard.

C. Zoom Chat and Whiteboard Integration

Zoom Whiteboard also integrates with Zoom Chat, allowing users to continue collaboration beyond meetings.

Ways to Use Zoom Whiteboard in Zoom Chat:

- Share whiteboards directly in a chat conversation.

- Allow team members to open and edit whiteboards without starting a meeting.

- Provide feedback by adding comments or annotations in a shared whiteboard.

Connecting Zoom Whiteboard with Productivity and Cloud Storage Tools

To maximize efficiency, many businesses and teams integrate Zoom Whiteboard with other popular productivity tools such as Google Workspace, Microsoft 365, and cloud storage platforms like Dropbox or OneDrive.

A. Google Workspace and Zoom Whiteboard

Integrating Google Drive, Docs, Sheets, and Slides with Zoom Whiteboard enables seamless document collaboration.

How to Integrate Google Workspace:

1. Enable Google Drive Integration in Zoom settings.

2. Share a whiteboard link in Google Docs or Google Chat for real-time collaboration.

3. Export whiteboard content as images or PDFs and upload them to Google Drive for storage.

B. Microsoft 365 and Zoom Whiteboard

For teams using Microsoft 365, Zoom Whiteboard can be integrated with OneDrive, Teams, and SharePoint to enhance workflow.

Benefits of Microsoft 365 Integration:

- Save and organize whiteboards in OneDrive for easy access.

- Use Zoom Whiteboard within Microsoft Teams for seamless communication.

- Embed whiteboards in SharePoint pages for team-wide collaboration.

C. Cloud Storage Solutions: Dropbox and OneDrive

Many teams rely on Dropbox and OneDrive for document storage. Integrating Zoom Whiteboard with these services helps with:

- Automatic backup of whiteboard files to prevent data loss.

- Easy access to previous whiteboards across different devices.

- Sharing whiteboards with team members who may not have access to Zoom.

Using APIs and Automation to Extend Zoom Whiteboard Capabilities

For businesses and tech-savvy users, Zoom offers APIs and automation tools to extend the functionality of Zoom Whiteboard.

A. Zoom API for Whiteboard Integration

Developers can use Zoom's API to create custom integrations between Zoom Whiteboard and other business tools.

Use Cases for Zoom API:

- Automatically generate whiteboards based on meeting topics.

- Sync whiteboard data with CRM systems like Salesforce.

- Create custom dashboards that display whiteboard activity and engagement metrics.

B. Zapier and Workflow Automation

For non-developers, tools like Zapier allow users to create automated workflows between Zoom Whiteboard and other apps.

Examples of Zapier Integrations:

- Save a new whiteboard to Google Drive or OneDrive automatically.

- Send notifications in Slack or Microsoft Teams when a whiteboard is updated.

- Convert whiteboard content into task lists in Trello or Asana.

Best Practices for Integrating Zoom Whiteboard with Other Tools

When integrating Zoom Whiteboard with third-party tools, keep the following best practices in mind:

1. Ensure Compatibility – Before integrating, check if your organization's tools support Zoom Whiteboard connections.

2. Maintain Security – Set up proper permissions when sharing whiteboards across platforms to prevent unauthorized access.

3. Standardize Naming Conventions – Use consistent file names and storage locations to avoid confusion when saving whiteboards.

4. Leverage Automation – Use APIs and workflow automation tools to reduce manual effort and enhance productivity.

5. Regularly Review and Update Integrations – Keep track of changes in software updates to maintain smooth integration.

Final Thoughts

Integrating Zoom Whiteboard with other Zoom features and third-party applications can significantly enhance collaboration, productivity, and workflow efficiency. Whether you're using Zoom Meetings, Google Workspace, Microsoft 365, or automation tools like Zapier, the ability to extend Zoom Whiteboard's capabilities ensures a seamless experience for individuals and teams alike.

By leveraging these integrations, users can maximize the potential of Zoom Whiteboard, making virtual collaboration more effective and engaging than ever before.

CHAPTER V
Use Cases and Real-World Applications

5.1 Business Meetings and Team Collaboration

5.1.1 Virtual Project Planning

Introduction to Virtual Project Planning with Zoom Whiteboard

In today's fast-paced and increasingly remote work environment, virtual project planning has become essential for businesses of all sizes. Traditional project planning methods—such as physical whiteboards, paper notes, and in-person meetings—are no longer practical for distributed teams. Zoom Whiteboard provides a powerful digital alternative that enables teams to visualize, collaborate, and organize project workflows in real time.

This section will explore how to effectively use Zoom Whiteboard for virtual project planning, covering essential techniques, best practices, and real-world applications. Whether you're a project manager, team leader, or business executive, mastering Zoom Whiteboard can significantly improve your team's efficiency and project execution.

Benefits of Using Zoom Whiteboard for Virtual Project Planning

1. Real-Time Collaboration from Anywhere

With Zoom Whiteboard, team members can collaborate in real time, regardless of location. This eliminates the need for in-person meetings and ensures that everyone stays aligned on project goals and tasks. Key benefits include:

- Instant Updates: Changes are reflected immediately, so there's no confusion about the latest project status.

- Seamless Remote Collaboration: Team members can contribute from anywhere, making it ideal for distributed teams.

- Reduced Miscommunication: Visualizing tasks and workflows ensures that all team members clearly understand their responsibilities.

2. Visual Representation of Workflows

Project planning often involves complex workflows that are difficult to manage using text-based tools. Zoom Whiteboard helps by:

- Creating Flowcharts to map out project stages and decision points.

- Using Kanban Boards for tracking task progress.

- Highlighting Dependencies to identify bottlenecks and streamline operations.

3. Easy Integration with Other Tools

Zoom Whiteboard integrates with various project management and collaboration tools, such as:

- Zoom Meetings (for discussing project updates).

- Trello, Asana, and Jira (for syncing task management).

- Google Drive and OneDrive (for document storage and sharing).

These integrations make it easier to manage projects without switching between multiple platforms.

Key Features of Zoom Whiteboard for Project Planning

1. Templates for Project Planning

Zoom Whiteboard offers built-in templates that simplify the process of project planning. Some useful templates include:

- Project Timeline Template – Helps teams map out milestones and deadlines.

- SWOT Analysis Template – Useful for evaluating strengths, weaknesses, opportunities, and threats.

- Brainstorming Template – Assists in idea generation and problem-solving.

Teams can also create and customize their own templates to fit specific project needs.

2. Sticky Notes and Comments for Task Assignments

Assigning tasks and responsibilities becomes more structured with the use of sticky notes and comments on Zoom Whiteboard:

- Sticky Notes can be used to create to-do lists and assign tasks to team members.

- Color Coding helps differentiate between urgent, pending, and completed tasks.

- Tagging Features allow managers to mention team members directly for task updates.

This method ensures that each team member knows their responsibilities and can track progress easily.

3. Layered Planning for Complex Projects

Large projects often involve multiple phases and sub-tasks. Zoom Whiteboard allows users to:

- Use Layers to separate different project components.

- Create Grouped Elements to organize related tasks and dependencies.

- Zoom In/Out to focus on specific project sections while maintaining a high-level overview.

This makes it easier to manage multi-stage projects without losing track of details.

Step-by-Step Guide to Using Zoom Whiteboard for Virtual Project Planning

Step 1: Setting Up the Whiteboard for Your Project

1. Open Zoom Whiteboard from your Zoom dashboard.

2. Select "New Whiteboard" and choose a suitable template (or start from scratch).

3. Define your project goals, timelines, and key milestones on the whiteboard.

Step 2: Structuring the Project Workflow

1. Use Flowcharts and Diagrams to break down the project into manageable steps.

2. Assign tasks to team members using sticky notes or text boxes.

3. Use color coding and icons to indicate task priority and status.

Step 3: Collaboration and Team Input

1. Share the whiteboard link with your team members.

2. Allow team members to add comments, suggestions, and updates.

3. Use Zoom Meetings to discuss updates while referring to the whiteboard.

Step 4: Tracking Progress and Making Adjustments

1. Review the status of each task during weekly check-ins.

2. Update milestones as needed and adjust deadlines accordingly.

3. Archive completed tasks and save different versions for future reference.

Best Practices for Virtual Project Planning with Zoom Whiteboard

1. Keep Your Whiteboard Organized

- Use clear labels and categories to differentiate tasks.

- Avoid clutter by grouping related elements together.

- Regularly clean up completed tasks to keep the board visually clear.

2. Establish a Collaboration Routine

- Set up regular meetings to review the whiteboard.

- Encourage team members to update the board frequently.

- Use notifications to keep everyone informed of changes.

3. Utilize Zoom's Additional Features

- Combine Zoom Whiteboard with Breakout Rooms for team discussions.

- Use Zoom Recording to document whiteboard brainstorming sessions.
- Share whiteboard exports via email or Slack for quick reference.

Real-World Example: Project Planning in a Remote Marketing Team

Imagine a remote marketing team planning a product launch. They use Zoom Whiteboard to:

1. Define Key Milestones – Campaign planning, content creation, ad launch, and review.
2. Assign Tasks – Team members take ownership of specific activities.
3. Monitor Progress – Weekly check-ins ensure everything stays on schedule.
4. Collaborate in Real-Time – Designers, writers, and advertisers refine ideas together.

By leveraging Zoom Whiteboard, the team keeps projects organized, avoids miscommunication, and meets deadlines efficiently.

Conclusion

Zoom Whiteboard revolutionizes virtual project planning by making it more interactive, structured, and accessible for remote teams. By utilizing templates, collaboration tools, and visual workflows, teams can improve productivity and communication.

Whether you're managing a marketing campaign, software development project, or strategic business initiative, Zoom Whiteboard ensures that your team stays aligned, engaged, and effective.

In the next section, we'll explore how Zoom Whiteboard can enhance education and remote learning, making virtual classrooms more engaging and interactive.

5.1.2 Agile and Scrum Workflows

Introduction to Agile and Scrum Workflows

Agile methodologies and Scrum frameworks have become essential for modern businesses looking to improve project management, streamline workflows, and increase team collaboration. Agile emphasizes iterative progress, flexibility, and customer collaboration, while Scrum is a structured framework that breaks projects into manageable increments called sprints.

Zoom Whiteboard plays a crucial role in enhancing Agile and Scrum processes, offering teams a virtual space to visualize, organize, and manage their tasks efficiently. Whether your team operates remotely or in a hybrid work environment, Zoom Whiteboard provides an intuitive and collaborative platform to conduct sprint planning, daily stand-ups, retrospectives, and backlog grooming sessions.

Benefits of Using Zoom Whiteboard for Agile and Scrum

1. Improved Team Collaboration

Zoom Whiteboard allows teams to collaborate in real-time, regardless of their location. Team members can brainstorm ideas, update tasks, and track project progress visually, ensuring everyone stays aligned on goals and priorities.

2. Enhanced Visualization of Workflows

Agile and Scrum methodologies rely on visual management tools such as Kanban boards and burn-down charts. Zoom Whiteboard provides customizable templates that make it easy to create and maintain these visual tools.

3. Increased Transparency and Accountability

By displaying the status of tasks, project goals, and team responsibilities, Zoom Whiteboard ensures that every team member understands their role and contributions. This transparency promotes accountability and minimizes miscommunication.

4. Seamless Integration with Zoom Meetings

Since Zoom Whiteboard is embedded in the Zoom ecosystem, teams can access their whiteboards directly during Zoom calls, making meetings more interactive and efficient.

This integration eliminates the need to switch between different applications, allowing for a seamless workflow.

How to Use Zoom Whiteboard in Scrum Workflows

1. Sprint Planning with Zoom Whiteboard

Sprint planning is a critical phase in Scrum, where the team defines what work will be completed in the upcoming sprint. Zoom Whiteboard enables teams to organize their sprint backlog visually, assign tasks, and prioritize features.

Steps to Conduct Sprint Planning Using Zoom Whiteboard:

1. **Create a Sprint Backlog Board**

   o Use a Kanban-style layout on Zoom Whiteboard to divide the sprint into categories such as "To Do," "In Progress," and "Completed."

   o Add sticky notes for user stories and tasks, assigning each to the relevant team members.

2. **Set Sprint Goals and Priorities**

   o Discuss the most critical user stories or features to be completed in the sprint.

   o Use Zoom Whiteboard's voting or annotation tools to prioritize items.

3. **Define Task Ownership**

   o Assign responsibilities by tagging team members on specific tasks.

   o Use color-coded labels to indicate different team roles (e.g., developers, testers, designers).

4. **Estimate Effort and Time Allocation**

   o Teams can use Zoom Whiteboard to perform **story point estimation**, using visual techniques like Planning Poker.

   o Drag-and-drop story points next to user stories to indicate complexity and estimated effort.

2. Daily Stand-Up Meetings with Zoom Whiteboard

Daily stand-ups are short meetings where team members provide updates on their work, discuss obstacles, and align their activities for the day.

How to Use Zoom Whiteboard for Daily Stand-Ups:

- Create a "Stand-Up Board" with three sections:
    1. What I did yesterday
    2. What I plan to do today
    3. Any blockers or challenges
- Each team member can add their updates using sticky notes or comments directly on the board.
- The Scrum Master can highlight blockers and assign follow-up actions in real time.

---

3. Sprint Review and Retrospective Using Zoom Whiteboard

At the end of each sprint, teams conduct a Sprint Review and a Sprint Retrospective.

Sprint Review: Showcasing Completed Work

- Use Zoom Whiteboard to present completed features and gather stakeholder feedback.
- Drag screenshots, links, or images onto the board to showcase deliverables.
- Enable real-time collaboration so that stakeholders can leave comments and suggestions.

Sprint Retrospective: Identifying Strengths and Areas for Improvement

- Create a "Retrospective Board" with three sections:
    o What went well?
    o What could be improved?
    o Action items for next sprint
- Team members can use sticky notes to provide feedback and suggestions.

- The Scrum Master can document insights and create follow-up tasks for the next sprint.

---

4. Backlog Grooming and Prioritization Using Zoom Whiteboard

Product backlog refinement (or grooming) is an ongoing process where teams review and update the backlog to ensure that upcoming tasks are well-defined and prioritized.

How to Use Zoom Whiteboard for Backlog Grooming:

1. **Organizing the Product Backlog**

   o Use a Kanban-style board to list all backlog items.

   o Sort tasks based on priority, urgency, or complexity.

2. **Clarifying User Stories**

   o Use text boxes and sticky notes to refine user stories, ensuring that they meet the Definition of Ready.

   o Tag product owners, developers, and designers to contribute their insights.

3. **Prioritization Techniques**

   o Apply prioritization frameworks like **MoSCoW (Must-Have, Should-Have, Could-Have, Won't-Have)** or **Value vs. Effort Matrix** using Zoom Whiteboard's diagramming tools.

Best Practices for Using Zoom Whiteboard in Agile and Scrum

1. Use Pre-Designed Templates

- Zoom Whiteboard offers templates for Scrum workflows, including Kanban boards, Sprint Planning, and Retrospective boards.

- Save custom templates to streamline recurring meetings.

2. Keep Boards Organized and Updated

- Regularly update the whiteboard to reflect real-time task progress.

- Archive completed sprints to maintain clarity and prevent clutter.

3. Encourage Team Participation

- Enable real-time commenting and annotations to make meetings more interactive.

- Assign facilitators to ensure engagement and structured discussions.

4. Integrate with Other Zoom and Project Management Tools

- Use Zoom Whiteboard alongside Jira, Trello, Asana, or Monday.com for more seamless backlog and sprint management.

- Export whiteboard content to PDF or other formats for easy sharing.

Conclusion

Zoom Whiteboard is a powerful tool that enhances Agile and Scrum workflows by providing a visual and interactive platform for sprint planning, daily stand-ups, backlog grooming, and retrospectives. Its seamless integration with Zoom Meetings makes it an essential tool for remote and hybrid teams looking to boost collaboration, transparency, and productivity.

By implementing the best practices outlined in this chapter, your team can maximize efficiency, improve communication, and drive successful project outcomes using Zoom Whiteboard.

5.1.3 Conducting Strategy Sessions

Strategic planning is the backbone of any successful organization. Whether you are developing a new business plan, setting company goals, or brainstorming market expansion strategies, Zoom Whiteboard can be an essential tool for conducting effective strategy sessions. By providing a dynamic and interactive space for team collaboration, it enhances communication, fosters creative problem-solving, and ensures that all team members are aligned on key objectives.

In this section, we will explore how to effectively use Zoom Whiteboard for strategy sessions, including preparation, facilitation, and follow-up strategies.

1. Preparing for a Strategy Session

A well-prepared strategy session can lead to productive discussions and actionable insights. Before launching into brainstorming, it's crucial to define objectives, set up the whiteboard properly, and ensure that all team members are aligned.

Defining Objectives and Agenda

- Clarify the Purpose: Every strategy session should have a clear goal. Are you identifying growth opportunities, analyzing competitors, or optimizing internal processes?

- Set the Agenda: Outline key discussion points and allocate time for each.

- Share Pre-Session Materials: Upload relevant documents, charts, and reports to Zoom Whiteboard so attendees can review them in advance.

Setting Up the Whiteboard for Maximum Engagement

- Choose the Right Template: Zoom Whiteboard offers pre-built strategy templates, such as SWOT Analysis, Business Model Canvas, and OKR (Objectives & Key Results) frameworks.

- Organize the Layout: Arrange sections on the whiteboard for brainstorming, prioritization, and final decisions.

- Use Color Codes: Assign different colors to different themes, teams, or decision categories for clarity.

Inviting the Right Participants

- Identify Key Stakeholders: Ensure that decision-makers and subject matter experts are involved.

- Encourage Pre-Session Input: Ask participants to add their initial thoughts to the whiteboard before the meeting starts.

- Set Collaboration Permissions: Configure Zoom Whiteboard's access levels—some participants may need full editing rights, while others may only need viewing access.

---

2. Running an Effective Strategy Session with Zoom Whiteboard

During the session, engagement and structured collaboration are key to making the most of Zoom Whiteboard's interactive features.

2.1 Facilitating Brainstorming and Idea Generation

- Use Sticky Notes for Idea Dumping: Encourage team members to add their thoughts using sticky notes.

- Enable Anonymous Contributions: Sometimes, anonymity can help generate more honest and creative input.

- Group Similar Ideas: Use smart connectors and grouping features to cluster related concepts.

2.2 Analyzing and Prioritizing Ideas

- Apply a Decision-Making Framework: Use proven methods like:

  - SWOT Analysis (Strengths, Weaknesses, Opportunities, Threats)

  - Eisenhower Matrix (Urgent vs. Important tasks)

  - MoSCoW Method (Must-have, Should-have, Could-have, Won't-have priorities)

- Utilize Voting Features: Have participants vote on the best ideas directly on the whiteboard.

- Draw Flowcharts for Decision Paths: Visually map out possible strategic directions.

2.3 Encouraging Real-Time Collaboration

- Assign Action Items on the Whiteboard: Create separate sections for responsibilities and due dates.

- Use Zoom's Chat & Audio Features: While discussing the whiteboard, leverage Zoom's built-in communication tools to ensure smooth discussions.

- Mark Progress with Visual Indicators: Use checkmarks, progress bars, and labels to track progress.

3. Wrapping Up and Ensuring Follow-Through

A strategy session is only successful if it leads to **clear action steps**. The final phase of the session should focus on capturing key takeaways and ensuring accountability.

3.1 Summarizing Key Decisions and Next Steps

- Highlight Final Agreements: Clearly document what decisions were made.

- Tag Responsible Team Members: Assign follow-up tasks directly on the whiteboard.

- Export the Whiteboard for Reference: Save and share the whiteboard as a PDF or image for future reference.

3.2 Scheduling Follow-Up Check-Ins

- Set Milestones for Progress Reviews: Use Zoom Calendar integration to schedule check-ins.

- Update the Whiteboard Continuously: Keep it as a living document that evolves over time.

- Encourage Feedback: Ask team members for suggestions on improving future strategy sessions.

4. Best Practices for Conducting Strategy Sessions with Zoom Whiteboard

To maximize the impact of your strategic meetings, consider the following best practices:

✅ **Encourage Visual Thinking** – Use diagrams, mind maps, and flowcharts to make complex ideas easier to understand.

✅ **Keep It Interactive** – Don't let one person dominate the discussion; ensure equal participation.

✅ **Balance Structure with Flexibility** – While a clear agenda is important, allow room for organic discussions.

✅ **Limit Session Length** – Keep strategy meetings concise (60-90 minutes) to maintain focus and energy.

✅ **Leverage AI and Automation** – Use AI-powered tools in Zoom Whiteboard to summarize discussions and suggest insights.

5. Conclusion

Using Zoom Whiteboard for strategy sessions enables organizations to enhance collaboration, make data-driven decisions, and drive innovation. By leveraging its interactive tools, real-time collaboration features, and structured frameworks, teams can visualize ideas more effectively and execute strategies with clarity.

As you continue using Zoom Whiteboard, explore new templates, integrations, and automation features to further refine your strategic planning process. The more familiar your team becomes with this tool, the more seamless and impactful your strategy sessions will be.

5.2 Education and Remote Learning

5.2.1 Teaching with Zoom Whiteboard

Introduction

The landscape of education has evolved dramatically with the rise of remote learning and digital collaboration tools. Zoom Whiteboard is a powerful feature that enables educators to create interactive and engaging lessons, enhancing student participation and understanding. Unlike traditional teaching methods, digital whiteboarding allows for dynamic visual explanations, real-time collaboration, and interactive learning experiences.

In this section, we will explore the advantages of using Zoom Whiteboard in teaching, practical strategies for implementation, and best practices to maximize its effectiveness in virtual classrooms.

Benefits of Using Zoom Whiteboard in Education

1. Enhancing Student Engagement

A major challenge in online learning is keeping students engaged. Zoom Whiteboard provides an interactive medium where teachers can visually present concepts, annotate in real-time, and encourage student participation through collaborative exercises. Features such as sticky notes, drawing tools, and image uploads make lessons more interactive and less monotonous.

2. Facilitating Real-Time Collaboration

Students can actively contribute to discussions by drawing, adding text, or sharing ideas on a shared whiteboard. This real-time interaction promotes active learning and teamwork, even in a virtual environment. Teachers can divide students into breakout rooms, assign collaborative tasks, and review their work instantly.

3. Supporting Different Learning Styles

Students have different learning preferences—some learn best through visuals, others through text, and some through hands-on practice. Zoom Whiteboard accommodates various learning styles by allowing teachers to integrate diagrams, charts, text-based explanations, and interactive problem-solving exercises in a single space.

4. Providing a Reusable and Accessible Learning Resource

Unlike physical whiteboards, Zoom Whiteboards can be saved, shared, and revisited by students after class. This is particularly useful for students who need additional time to review lessons or for those who missed a session. Teachers can also prepare whiteboards in advance and modify them as needed.

How to Effectively Use Zoom Whiteboard for Teaching

1. Preparing and Structuring the Whiteboard Content

Before starting a class, it's essential to have a well-structured whiteboard setup. Here are some key steps:

- **Plan the Layout**: Decide in advance what content will be presented. Use different sections or layers to organize information clearly.

- **Use Templates**: Zoom Whiteboard offers various templates that can be customized for different subjects and lesson plans.

- **Integrate Visual Aids**: Enhance explanations with images, graphs, and charts to make complex topics easier to understand.

- **Pre-fill Key Information**: Instead of writing everything in real-time, prepare key points ahead of time to save time and focus on discussions.

2. Conducting an Interactive Lesson with Zoom Whiteboard

Once the whiteboard is ready, teachers can use different techniques to make lessons engaging:

2.1 Live Annotations and Explanations

- Use the **pen and highlighter tools** to emphasize key points.

- Write down students' responses directly on the whiteboard to make discussions feel interactive.

- Draw diagrams in real time to visually explain abstract concepts, such as mathematical equations or scientific processes.

2.2 Student Participation and Collaboration

- Allow students to contribute by enabling editing access.

- Assign group tasks where students add their ideas using sticky notes or drawing tools.

- Encourage students to solve problems together by completing fill-in-the-blank exercises, labeling diagrams, or brainstorming on a shared whiteboard.

2.3 Breakout Room Activities

Zoom's breakout rooms work seamlessly with Whiteboard, allowing smaller groups of students to collaborate on specific tasks. Teachers can:

- Assign different groups to solve a case study and present their findings using a shared whiteboard.

- Have students draft storyboards for creative writing exercises.

- Use flowcharts to illustrate problem-solving processes.

3. Managing and Organizing Multiple Whiteboards

During a lesson, multiple whiteboards may be needed for different topics or activities. Teachers can:

- Create separate whiteboards for different lesson segments (e.g., theory, exercises, and Q&A).

- Use **naming conventions** to keep whiteboards organized and easy to reference later.

- Save whiteboards for future use and allow students to revisit them for review.

Practical Use Cases for Different Subjects

1. Science and Mathematics

Zoom Whiteboard is particularly effective for subjects that require visual demonstrations. Teachers can:

- Draw and label scientific diagrams (e.g., the human body, cell structures, or physics circuits).

- Solve step-by-step math problems, showing equations and calculations in real time.
- Use graphs and charts to illustrate statistical data or experimental results.

2. Language and Literature

For language classes, Zoom Whiteboard can facilitate:

- Interactive grammar exercises, where students correct sentences or rearrange words.
- Storyboarding activities to plan narratives or analyze literature.
- Vocabulary-building activities using images and word association maps.

3. History and Social Studies

Teachers can:

- Create timelines of historical events with student contributions.
- Use maps to discuss geographical locations and historical battles.
- Organize debate topics and record key points using collaborative mind maps.

Best Practices for Teaching with Zoom Whiteboard

To ensure the most effective use of Zoom Whiteboard in online classrooms, consider these best practices:

1. Keep It Simple and Clear

- Avoid cluttering the whiteboard with too much information.
- Use different colors for clarity but avoid excessive visual distractions.

2. Set Guidelines for Student Contributions

- Establish rules on how students should use the whiteboard (e.g., taking turns, using designated sections).
- Assign specific roles (e.g., one student writes, another organizes content).

3. Utilize Whiteboard Tools Effectively

- Use layers to separate background elements from student contributions.

- Leverage keyboard shortcuts to streamline writing and navigation.

- Integrate multimedia elements (images, videos, or links) to enhance understanding.

4. Encourage Active Participation

- Ask students to interact with the whiteboard every few minutes to maintain engagement.

- Use questions and prompts to guide discussions.

- Provide immediate feedback through annotations and comments.

Conclusion

Teaching with Zoom Whiteboard transforms remote learning into an interactive, dynamic, and engaging experience. By leveraging its collaborative features, teachers can create visually appealing lessons, encourage student participation, and enhance learning retention.

To maximize its potential, educators should structure whiteboard content strategically, integrate interactive exercises, and establish clear guidelines for collaboration. With proper implementation, Zoom Whiteboard becomes more than just a digital tool—it becomes a virtual classroom that fosters creativity, critical thinking, and teamwork among students.

By continuously exploring new ways to use Zoom Whiteboard, teachers can make online education more effective, ensuring that students remain engaged and inspired in their learning journey.

5.2.2 Engaging Students with Interactive Exercises

Introduction

In today's digital learning environment, student engagement is a critical factor in effective education. Traditional lectures often fail to capture students' attention, especially in remote learning settings where distractions abound. Zoom Whiteboard offers a dynamic and interactive way to enhance student participation, promote collaboration, and foster creativity.

This section explores how educators can leverage Zoom Whiteboard to create interactive exercises, covering different types of activities, step-by-step implementation guides, and best practices for maximizing engagement.

1. The Importance of Interactivity in Learning

Studies have shown that students retain information better when they actively engage with the learning material. Interactivity enhances comprehension, encourages critical thinking, and improves retention rates.

With Zoom Whiteboard, instructors can transform passive learning into an active experience. Instead of simply delivering lectures, they can encourage students to collaborate, brainstorm, and visualize ideas in real-time.

Key Benefits of Interactive Exercises with Zoom Whiteboard:

✓ Enhances student participation – Active involvement keeps students motivated.
✓ Supports different learning styles – Visual learners benefit from diagrams, while kinesthetic learners engage through interactive drawing and annotation.
✓ Promotes teamwork and collaboration – Students can work together on group projects or problem-solving activities.
✓ Encourages creativity and critical thinking – Open-ended exercises help students explore and develop ideas independently.

2. Types of Interactive Exercises Using Zoom Whiteboard

2.1 Brainstorming Activities

Encouraging students to generate ideas and collaborate in real-time fosters creativity.

How to Implement:

- Create a blank whiteboard and divide it into sections for different topics or groups.

- Ask students to contribute keywords, phrases, or images related to a topic.

- Use sticky notes or text boxes to organize their ideas into categories.

- Have students connect related ideas using arrows or lines.

💡 *Example:* In a history class, students brainstorm causes and effects of historical events, grouping them into categories like political, social, and economic factors.

2.2 Concept Mapping and Mind Maps

A mind map is a visual tool that helps students organize information logically.

How to Implement:

- Start with a central concept in the middle of the whiteboard.

- Have students add branches representing subtopics or key points.

- Use colors, icons, and images to differentiate ideas.

- Encourage students to explain connections between concepts.

💡 *Example:* In a biology class, students create a mind map on ecosystems, linking components like producers, consumers, and decomposers.

2.3 Interactive Quizzes and Polls

Quizzes can be fun and engaging, reinforcing learning through immediate feedback.

How to Implement:

- Use Zoom Whiteboard to create a multiple-choice question template.

- Students mark their answers using sticky notes, drawing tools, or color-coded markers.

- Discuss the correct answers as a group and encourage peer explanations.

💡 *Example:* In a language class, teachers can display scrambled sentences and have students rearrange them in the correct order using Zoom Whiteboard tools.

2.4 Collaborative Problem-Solving

Students learn best by solving problems together, applying their knowledge in a practical context.

How to Implement:

- Present a real-world scenario or challenge on the whiteboard.

- Divide students into small groups and assign each group a section of the whiteboard.

- Allow students to write down their solutions using text boxes, drawings, or equations.

- Have groups present their ideas and discuss alternative solutions.

💡 *Example:* In a math class, different groups solve sections of a complex equation step-by-step on the whiteboard.

2.5 Drawing and Diagramming Activities

Drawing can be an effective tool for visual learners.

How to Implement:

- Provide a partially completed diagram and ask students to fill in missing parts.

- Have students illustrate concepts using drawing tools.

- Use the sticky note feature to let students add explanations to their drawings.

💡 *Example:* In a geography class, students label continents and oceans on a world map drawn on Zoom Whiteboard.

---

3. Best Practices for Using Zoom Whiteboard in Education

3.1 Setting Clear Instructions

- Explain the goal of the exercise before starting.

- Demonstrate how to use Zoom Whiteboard tools.

- Provide a time limit to keep students focused.

3.2 Encouraging Collaboration and Peer Learning

- Assign specific roles to students (e.g., note-taker, presenter, researcher).

- Allow students to comment on each other's contributions.

- Use the version history feature to track progress and edits.

3.3 Keeping Engagement High

- Use colorful visuals and interactive elements.

- Integrate games and challenges into lessons.

- Rotate students through different roles to keep participation levels high.

4. Case Study: Real-World Example of Zoom Whiteboard in Education

Scenario: Online Science Class

A high school science teacher uses Zoom Whiteboard to teach the water cycle.

Step-by-Step Approach:

1. The teacher displays a blank water cycle diagram on Zoom Whiteboard.

2. Students take turns labeling different parts (evaporation, condensation, precipitation).

3. The teacher adds real-world examples (e.g., how rainfall affects agriculture).

4. Students form groups to create mini-presentations explaining each stage.

5. The teacher reviews and provides feedback using annotation tools.

Results:
✅ Students demonstrated a better understanding of the water cycle.
✅ Engagement levels were higher compared to traditional lecture-based teaching.
✅ The activity fostered collaboration and critical thinking.

5. Conclusion and Next Steps

Zoom Whiteboard provides educators with a powerful tool to create engaging and interactive learning experiences. By incorporating brainstorming activities, quizzes, problem-solving tasks, and visual diagrams, teachers can keep students motivated and actively involved.

To further enhance student engagement, educators should:

✓ Experiment with different types of exercises to find what works best for their students.

✓ Encourage students to take ownership of the whiteboard space.

✓ Continuously adapt exercises based on student feedback and learning outcomes.

By making lessons interactive and visually engaging, teachers can unlock the full potential of remote learning and create a more meaningful educational experience.

5.2.3 Online Tutoring and Training Workshops

Introduction

Online tutoring and training workshops have revolutionized the way individuals learn and develop new skills. Whether for academic tutoring, corporate training, or professional development, digital whiteboards have become essential tools for interactive teaching. Zoom Whiteboard provides a powerful platform for educators, trainers, and coaches to engage learners, collaborate visually, and enhance knowledge retention.

In this section, we will explore how Zoom Whiteboard can be effectively utilized for one-on-one tutoring, group training sessions, and corporate workshops. We will also discuss best practices, essential tools, and strategies for making virtual learning sessions engaging and productive.

Benefits of Using Zoom Whiteboard for Online Tutoring

1. Real-Time Collaboration

Zoom Whiteboard allows tutors and students to interact in real-time, making the learning process more dynamic. Unlike traditional slide presentations, which are often static, whiteboards provide a free-form workspace where tutors can illustrate concepts, work through problems, and visually explain difficult topics.

For example, a math tutor can use the pen tool to solve equations step-by-step, while a language tutor can use the text tool to highlight sentence structures and grammar rules.

2. Engaging Visual Learning

Many students learn better when information is presented visually. The use of diagrams, charts, and mind maps helps break down complex concepts into digestible pieces. Tutors can use:

- Sticky notes for key takeaways

- Shapes and connectors for concept mapping

- Embedded images and PDFs for reference materials

For instance, a science tutor explaining the water cycle can draw a diagram on the whiteboard, label the different stages, and use arrows to show the flow of the process.

3. Interactive Exercises and Assessments

Zoom Whiteboard enables tutors to create interactive learning activities such as:

- Fill-in-the-blank exercises using text boxes

- Drag-and-drop activities for categorizing concepts

- Live brainstorming sessions with students

Trainers can also record whiteboard sessions for students to review later, ensuring they can revisit key concepts at their own pace.

4. Easy Access and Integration with Other Tools

Since Zoom Whiteboard is integrated into the Zoom ecosystem, students and tutors don't need additional software. The whiteboard is accessible across multiple devices, including laptops, tablets, and even smartphones. Additionally, Zoom Whiteboard integrates with Google Drive, OneDrive, and Dropbox, making it easy to import study materials and share them with students.

Conducting Effective Online Tutoring Sessions

1. Setting Up Your Virtual Classroom

Before starting an online tutoring session, ensure that:

✓ Your Zoom settings allow screen sharing and whiteboard access

✓ Students have permission to annotate and interact with the whiteboard

✓ Necessary materials (diagrams, worksheets, PDFs) are preloaded

To create a structured lesson, consider using pre-designed templates for different subjects. For example:

- A math template with a grid background for geometry lessons

- A writing template with lined sections for essay structuring

- A mind map template for brainstorming and organizing ideas

2. Engaging Students with Interactive Activities

To maintain student engagement, use a mix of direct instruction and interactive participation. Here are some strategies:

✓ Annotation Challenges – Have students highlight important points or solve problems directly on the whiteboard.

✓ Live Polling and Q&A – Use sticky notes or comments to collect student responses.

✓ Timed Exercises – Set a timer on the whiteboard for quick problem-solving drills.

For example, in a language tutoring session, the tutor can write sentence fragments on sticky notes and ask students to rearrange them into grammatically correct sentences.

3. Recording and Reviewing Sessions

Zoom allows tutors to record sessions, including whiteboard activities, for later review. After the session, tutors can:

- Share the whiteboard file with students for reference

- Provide homework assignments based on the session's content

- Analyze whiteboard notes to track student progress over time

This feature is especially useful for corporate training, where employees might need to revisit sessions for reinforcement.

Using Zoom Whiteboard for Corporate Training Workshops

1. Virtual Skill Development Workshops

Zoom Whiteboard is widely used in professional training sessions to:
✓ Facilitate brainstorming for leadership development
✓ Illustrate business strategies using flowcharts
✓ Conduct team-building exercises with interactive activities

For instance, in a corporate finance workshop, trainers can use charting tools to explain revenue models and financial forecasting.

2. Hands-On Training with Real-World Scenarios

One of the most effective ways to train employees is through simulated exercises. Trainers can create realistic scenarios on Zoom Whiteboard, such as:

- Role-playing exercises for customer service training

- Decision-making simulations for business management courses

- Project planning exercises for Agile methodology workshops

For example, in a project management training session, trainers can create a Kanban board on Zoom Whiteboard, where participants move tasks through different workflow stages.

3. Team Collaboration and Group Exercises

Corporate training workshops often involve team-based activities, such as:
✓ Group brainstorming sessions for product innovation
✓ SWOT analysis exercises for strategic planning
✓ Problem-solving challenges to develop critical thinking

A marketing team workshop, for instance, could use mind mapping tools to generate ideas for a new advertising campaign, with different team members contributing in real-time.

Best Practices for Successful Online Training and Tutoring

1. Keep Sessions Interactive

Avoid long lectures—engage participants with frequent activities and discussion prompts.

2. Use a Structured Approach

Clearly outline learning objectives at the start and provide a roadmap for the session.

3. Incorporate Multimedia Elements

Use images, videos, and links to external resources to enhance engagement.

4. Encourage Student Participation

Allow students to take control of the whiteboard and express their ideas visually.

5. Follow Up with Learning Materials

After the session, share the whiteboard file, additional reading materials, and assignments to reinforce learning.

Conclusion

Zoom Whiteboard is a game-changer for online tutoring and corporate training, offering a dynamic and engaging way to teach, brainstorm, and collaborate. By leveraging real-time interaction, visual tools, and structured learning techniques, tutors and trainers can deliver high-quality education and professional development experiences.

Whether you're a private tutor, an educator, or a corporate trainer, mastering Zoom Whiteboard will elevate your ability to connect with learners, enhance comprehension, and create a more interactive virtual learning environment.

5.3 Creative and Design Work

5.3.1 Wireframing and UI/UX Design

In today's digital landscape, wireframing and UI/UX (User Interface/User Experience) design are essential steps in the development of websites, applications, and digital products. These processes help designers visualize and refine the structure, layout, and user interactions before moving into full development. Zoom Whiteboard provides an intuitive and collaborative platform for UI/UX designers to sketch ideas, create wireframes, and gather feedback in real time.

In this section, we will explore how Zoom Whiteboard can be used for wireframing and UI/UX design, including:

- Understanding wireframing and UI/UX design principles

- Using Zoom Whiteboard tools for wireframing

- Collaborating with teams on UX design projects

- Gathering feedback and iterating on designs

- Best practices for maximizing efficiency

1. Understanding Wireframing and UI/UX Design Principles

Before diving into how to use Zoom Whiteboard for UI/UX work, it's crucial to understand wireframing and its role in the UI/UX design process.

What Is Wireframing?

A wireframe is a visual guide that represents the skeletal structure of a webpage or application. It focuses on layout, functionality, and content placement without including detailed design elements like colors, images, or final typography.

Why Are Wireframes Important?

Wireframing plays a critical role in UI/UX design by:

- Clarifying structure and functionality before investing in high-fidelity designs.

- Providing a blueprint for developers, ensuring alignment between designers and engineers.

- Identifying usability issues early, reducing costly revisions later.

- Facilitating client and stakeholder approvals with a clear visual representation.

2. Using Zoom Whiteboard Tools for Wireframing

Setting Up Your Whiteboard for Wireframing

1. Create a New Whiteboard: Open Zoom Whiteboard and set up a blank canvas.

2. Define a Grid System: Use rulers, guidelines, or the grid background to maintain alignment.

3. Use Shapes and Lines: Basic UI elements like buttons, input fields, menus, and containers can be created using rectangles, circles, and lines.

4. Add Text Labels: Use text boxes to indicate navigation items, placeholders, or descriptions.

5. Utilize Sticky Notes: Label elements with additional notes for clarity.

Key Zoom Whiteboard Tools for Wireframing

Tool	Use Case in Wireframing
Shapes (Rectangles, Circles, Lines)	Creating UI elements like buttons, navigation bars, forms, and containers.
Sticky Notes	Adding contextual information or notes for team members.
Text Tool	Labeling interface components.
Smart Connectors	Linking elements to show navigation flow.
Templates	Reusing pre-made UI components.
Image Uploads	Importing reference images or brand assets.

3. Collaborating with Teams on UX Design Projects

One of Zoom Whiteboard's greatest advantages is its ability to support real-time collaboration among designers, developers, and stakeholders.

How to Collaborate Effectively

- Invite Team Members: Grant edit/view access to designers, product managers, and developers.

- Use Live Annotation: Team members can add comments, suggest changes, and highlight areas directly on the wireframe.

- Leverage Version History: Easily track changes and revert to previous versions when needed.

- Assign Colors for Roles: Use different colors for design suggestions, user feedback, and developer notes.

Real-World Collaboration Scenarios

Scenario	How Zoom Whiteboard Helps
Design Sprints	Quickly sketch wireframes and iterate in real-time.
Client Reviews	Share a live board with clients for instant feedback.
Developer Handoffs	Provide annotations and detailed explanations of UI elements.

4. Gathering Feedback and Iterating on Designs

In UI/UX design, gathering early feedback and making quick iterations is key to delivering a user-friendly product.

Using Zoom Whiteboard for Feedback Collection

1. **Commenting and Annotation**:
   - Team members can leave sticky notes or comments on specific UI elements.

2. **Voting on Design Choices**:
   - Use emoji reactions or mark elements that need changes.

3. **Version Comparison**:

   o   Save multiple versions and compare different iterations.

4. **User Testing Notes**:

   o   Document usability testing results directly on the board.

Example Feedback Workflow

1. Create a wireframe on Zoom Whiteboard.

2. Share the board with team members.

3. Collect feedback through annotations.

4. Make changes based on the suggestions.

5. Repeat the process until a final version is approved.

5. Best Practices for Maximizing Efficiency

Organizing Wireframes for Large Projects

- Use Separate Sections: Divide your whiteboard into sections (e.g., homepage, dashboard, checkout flow).

- Create a UI Library: Store reusable components for faster wireframing.

- Label Versions Clearly: Indicate iteration numbers (e.g., "Homepage V1", "Dashboard V3").

Leveraging Integrations with Other Tools

Zoom Whiteboard can be used alongside other design tools for a seamless workflow:

Tool	Integration Purpose
Figma	Import high-fidelity UI designs for comparison.
Adobe XD	Export wireframes for further prototyping.
Google Docs	Store UX research notes and documentation.

Tool	Integration Purpose
Trello / Jira	Attach wireframes to project management tasks.

Time-Saving Tips for UI/UX Designers

✓ Use keyboard shortcuts to speed up wireframing.

✓ Pre-build common UI components to reuse across projects.

✓ Limit distractions by using focus mode during design sessions.

✓ Encourage async collaboration by allowing team members to leave notes at different times.

Conclusion

Zoom Whiteboard is a powerful tool for wireframing and UI/UX design, offering an easy-to-use, collaborative environment where teams can sketch, iterate, and refine designs in real time. By following best practices and utilizing Zoom Whiteboard's drawing tools, smart connectors, feedback collection, and integrations, designers can accelerate their workflow, enhance collaboration, and create user-friendly interfaces efficiently.

Whether you're a solo designer, working with a small team, or part of a large enterprise UX department, mastering Zoom Whiteboard can transform the way you brainstorm, wireframe, and bring ideas to life.

5.3.2 Storyboarding for Media and Marketing

Storyboarding is an essential tool in media production and marketing campaigns, helping teams visualize ideas, streamline workflows, and enhance collaboration. With Zoom Whiteboard, professionals can create, modify, and share storyboards in real time, making it easier than ever to plan videos, advertisements, presentations, and more.

In this section, we'll explore how Zoom Whiteboard can be effectively used for storyboarding in media and marketing, covering the fundamentals of storyboarding, key features of Zoom Whiteboard, best practices, and real-world applications.

---

1. Understanding Storyboarding in Media and Marketing

What is Storyboarding?

Storyboarding is a visual planning process that outlines a sequence of events in a narrative, typically using illustrations, sketches, or images. In media and marketing, storyboarding is crucial for:

- Video production – planning scenes for commercials, explainer videos, and brand storytelling.

- Marketing campaigns – mapping out customer journeys, social media content, and ad placements.

- Presentation development – structuring key messages for product pitches and promotional materials.

- Animation and motion graphics – designing frames for digital ads, corporate animations, and training videos.

Benefits of Storyboarding in Media and Marketing

Using storyboarding in media and marketing projects provides several advantages:

- Clarity and organization – Visualizing ideas helps align teams and stakeholders.

- Efficient planning – Saves time by mapping out content before production.

- Improved collaboration – Allows input from designers, writers, and marketing teams.

- Better storytelling – Ensures a logical and engaging narrative flow.

2. Using Zoom Whiteboard for Storyboarding

Zoom Whiteboard offers an interactive digital canvas that enables teams to create and refine storyboards collaboratively. Here's how you can leverage its features:

Setting Up a Storyboard in Zoom Whiteboard

To start a storyboard in Zoom Whiteboard:

1. Create a new Whiteboard – Open Zoom Whiteboard from the Zoom Web Portal or directly from a Zoom Meeting.

2. Set up a template – Use pre-designed frames for consistent panel structures.

3. Add a grid layout – Structure scenes with rectangular frames for each step in the storyboard.

4. Define key elements – Use shapes, sticky notes, and text boxes to describe shots, actions, and dialogues.

Essential Tools for Storyboarding

Zoom Whiteboard includes a range of tools that enhance the storyboarding process:

- Drawing Tools – Sketch rough concepts using the pen, highlighter, and eraser.

- Shapes and Frames – Create structured panels for different scenes.

- Sticky Notes – Add quick descriptions, scene notes, or dialogue cues.

- Image and Video Upload – Insert screenshots, reference images, or thumbnails from existing projects.

- Smart Connectors – Link elements together to illustrate motion, transitions, or interactions.

- Commenting and Feedback – Team members can leave notes, suggest changes, and approve designs.

Collaborating on Storyboards in Real-Time

One of the biggest advantages of Zoom Whiteboard is its real-time collaboration:

- Invite team members to contribute to the storyboard.

- Assign roles (e.g., designer, copywriter, editor) for efficient workflow.

- Use version history to track changes and revisions.

- Integrate with Zoom Meetings to discuss adjustments while working on the storyboard.

3. Best Practices for Storyboarding with Zoom Whiteboard

Structuring a Storyboard for Maximum Clarity

- Use consistent panel sizes to maintain a professional layout.

- Arrange scenes in chronological order for clear storytelling.

- Keep text brief – use simple descriptions rather than long explanations.

- Differentiate backgrounds and foregrounds using color coding.

Making the Storyboard Interactive

- Add clickable elements for interactive storytelling.

- Use arrows and flowcharts to indicate movement between frames.

- Embed links to reference materials for deeper context.

Improving Team Collaboration

- Schedule live editing sessions in Zoom Meetings.

- Use the chat feature to discuss specific scenes.

- Encourage feedback using color-coded annotations.

4. Real-World Applications of Storyboarding in Marketing

Video Advertising

Zoom Whiteboard helps marketing teams storyboard TV commercials, YouTube ads, and social media video content by:

- Mapping out key scenes and transitions.
- Aligning visual elements with voiceovers and sound effects.
- Ensuring consistent brand messaging across multiple platforms.

Social Media Campaigns

For platforms like Instagram, TikTok, and LinkedIn, storyboarding helps:

- Plan carousel posts, story sequences, and short video clips.
- Define call-to-action (CTA) placements.
- Organize content themes and branding visuals.

Website and Landing Page Design

Marketers can use Zoom Whiteboard to:

- Sketch website wireframes.
- Plan user journeys and conversion funnels.
- Collaborate with designers on banner layouts and interactive elements.

Email Marketing and Presentation Planning

- Design story-driven email sequences for product launches.
- Structure sales pitches and investor presentations.
- Align visual storytelling with copywriting.

5. Conclusion: Transforming Marketing with Zoom Whiteboard

Using Zoom Whiteboard for storyboarding revolutionizes the way media and marketing teams visualize, plan, and execute their creative ideas. Whether for advertising, social media, presentations, or website design, storyboarding helps streamline workflows and improve collaboration.

By mastering Zoom Whiteboard's tools, real-time features, and best practices, marketing professionals can enhance their storytelling capabilities, drive engagement, and execute more effective campaigns.

5.3.3 Collaborative Art and Concept Sketching

Introduction

In today's digital world, artists, designers, and creative professionals are increasingly embracing online collaboration tools to streamline their workflows and enhance teamwork. Zoom Whiteboard provides an intuitive and versatile platform for artists, illustrators, and concept designers to collaborate in real time, regardless of their physical locations.

This section explores how creative teams can leverage Zoom Whiteboard for collaborative art and concept sketching, covering its essential tools, best practices, and real-world applications. Whether you are a graphic designer, storyboard artist, UX/UI designer, or illustrator, understanding how to integrate Zoom Whiteboard into your creative process can boost productivity and foster innovation.

Understanding the Benefits of Zoom Whiteboard for Art Collaboration

1. Real-Time Collaboration from Anywhere

One of the biggest advantages of using Zoom Whiteboard for art and sketching is the ability to collaborate in real time with artists, designers, and clients worldwide. This feature is particularly useful for:

- Creative teams working remotely on the same project.

- Design agencies that need quick feedback from clients.

- Freelancers and independent artists who want to work with other creators without physical constraints.

2. Seamless Integration with Other Creative Tools

Artists often rely on software like Adobe Photoshop, Illustrator, Procreate, and Figma. While Zoom Whiteboard is not a replacement for these tools, it can complement them in multiple ways:

- Initial concept sketching before refining designs in advanced software.

- Gathering feedback and making real-time revisions before moving to final production.

- Using the whiteboard as a collaborative mood board for brainstorming ideas.

3. Simplified Workflow for Concept Sketching

Instead of relying on lengthy email chains or static PDFs, artists can use Zoom Whiteboard to:

- Quickly sketch out ideas using the built-in drawing tools.

- Organize different design concepts using layers and grouping elements.

- Annotate and highlight design elements for easy collaboration.

Essential Zoom Whiteboard Tools for Collaborative Art

1. Drawing and Freehand Sketching

The pen and highlighter tools in Zoom Whiteboard allow artists to:

- Sketch rough ideas and refine them over time.

- Use different colors to differentiate elements.

- Highlight important areas for discussion.

2. Shape and Line Tools

While freehand sketching is essential for artistic expression, structured designs often require precise shapes and lines:

- Circles and rectangles for UI/UX wireframing.

- Straight lines and arrows to show motion or relationships between elements.

- Flowchart connectors for interactive design elements.

3. Sticky Notes and Text Annotations

Adding sticky notes allows teams to:

- Provide quick feedback on specific parts of the sketch.

- Brainstorm new ideas related to the current artwork.

- Annotate sketches with layer names, colors, or action items.

4. Image Uploads and Reference Boards

Artists can import images, textures, and references to:

- Use mood boards for inspiration.

- Overlay sketches on existing designs.

- Compare different versions of artwork in real time.

5. Version Control and Layer Management

To stay organized, teams can:

- Use layers to separate elements (e.g., foreground, background, text).

- Save different versions of the sketch to track changes.

- Undo and redo actions without losing progress.

Best Practices for Collaborative Sketching in Zoom Whiteboard

1. Set Clear Objectives Before Starting

Before jumping into the sketching process, ensure that everyone is aligned on:

- The purpose of the whiteboard session.

- The style and direction of the artwork.

- The roles of each participant (e.g., lead artist, reviewer, contributor).

2. Use a Structured Layout

To keep the whiteboard organized:

- Allocate specific areas for different concepts.

- Use grids or guides for alignment.

- Group related sketches together to avoid confusion.

3. Establish a Feedback Loop

Encourage participants to:

- Use sticky notes for non-intrusive comments.

- Mark sections needing revisions with highlights or shapes.

- Provide constructive criticism rather than vague feedback.

4. Save and Export Regularly

Since whiteboards are dynamic, it's crucial to:

- Save snapshots at different stages of the design.

- Export final sketches in PNG, PDF, or SVG formats.

- Keep backups in Google Drive, Dropbox, or OneDrive.

5. Combine Zoom Whiteboard with Live Video Calls

For better communication and faster decision-making:

- Discuss sketches via Zoom's video and audio features.

- Share screens for side-by-side comparisons with external software.

- Use Breakout Rooms for separate discussion groups.

Real-World Use Cases of Zoom Whiteboard for Artists

1. Concept Art and Storyboarding for Film & Animation

Film directors, storyboard artists, and animators can use Zoom Whiteboard to:

- Sketch out storyboard sequences for movies and animations.

- Visualize character movements and scene compositions.

- Collaborate with writers, directors, and voice actors.

2. UX/UI Wireframing for App and Web Design

Product designers and developers use Zoom Whiteboard for:

- Wireframing and prototyping new app interfaces.

- Gathering live feedback from stakeholders.

- Iterating designs before moving to Figma or Adobe XD.

3. Graphic Design and Branding Workshops

Marketing teams and designers collaborate on:

- Logo design brainstorming with quick sketching.

- Creating visual identity concepts for brands.

- Finalizing typography and color palettes with client feedback.

4. Game Design and Character Development

Game developers and artists can use Zoom Whiteboard to:

- Sketch initial character designs and environments.

- Plan out game levels and mechanics visually.

- Work with writers and developers on world-building.

Conclusion

Collaborative sketching on Zoom Whiteboard offers a flexible, accessible, and efficient way for artists, designers, and creative teams to work together seamlessly in real time. With the right tools and best practices, teams can brainstorm, refine, and finalize designs faster than ever before.

By combining Zoom Whiteboard with other digital design tools, creative professionals can enhance their workflows, improve feedback loops, and produce high-quality visual content efficiently. Whether you're sketching concepts, developing UI/UX wireframes, or storyboarding for a film, mastering Zoom Whiteboard will give you a powerful edge in the world of digital collaboration.

CHAPTER VI
Troubleshooting and Future Trends

6.1 Common Issues and How to Fix Them

6.1.1 Connectivity and Sync Problems

Zoom Whiteboard is a powerful tool for collaboration, but like any cloud-based platform, it can occasionally encounter connectivity and synchronization issues. These problems can disrupt workflows, cause delays, and lead to frustration among users. This section will explore common connectivity and sync problems, their potential causes, and step-by-step solutions to resolve them effectively.

Understanding Connectivity and Sync Problems

Connectivity issues with Zoom Whiteboard typically arise due to:

- **Network instability** – Weak or intermittent internet connections can disrupt real-time collaboration.

- **Firewall and security settings** – Some organizations restrict Zoom services, blocking access to Whiteboard features.

- **Outdated software or browser** – Older versions of Zoom or unsupported browsers may prevent smooth syncing.

- **Cloud storage delays** – Since Zoom Whiteboard is cloud-based, occasional server-side delays can affect updates.

Sync problems often involve:

- **Delayed updates** – Changes made by one user are not immediately visible to others.

- **Missing content** – Some elements may disappear or fail to save correctly.

- **Multiple versions of the same whiteboard** – If sync fails, users may accidentally create conflicting copies.

Troubleshooting Connectivity Issues

1. Checking Internet Connection

A stable internet connection is essential for Zoom Whiteboard to function smoothly. Follow these steps to diagnose and improve connectivity:

- **Test your speed**: Ensure you have at least **10 Mbps download and 5 Mbps upload speed** for smooth collaboration.
    - Use online tools like Speedtest.net to check your internet speed.

- **Switch to a wired connection**: If possible, use an Ethernet cable instead of Wi-Fi to avoid wireless interference.

- **Reduce network congestion**:
    - Close unnecessary apps that consume bandwidth (e.g., video streaming, large file downloads).
    - Ask others in your household or office to limit heavy internet usage during meetings.

- **Restart your modem/router**:
    - Unplug your router for **30 seconds** and restart it.
    - If using a corporate network, contact your IT team for assistance.

2. Ensuring Zoom Whiteboard is Not Blocked

Some company or school networks restrict Zoom Whiteboard. To check and resolve this:

- **Verify with IT**: Ask your IT department if Zoom Whiteboard is permitted on the network.

- **Adjust firewall settings**:

    - Allow **Zoom-related domains and ports** in your firewall settings.

    - Open required ports (TCP 443 and UDP 3478-3497) for Zoom's cloud services.

- **Try a different network**: If possible, switch to a personal hotspot or another Wi-Fi network to see if the issue persists.

3. Updating Zoom and Browser

Using outdated software can cause Whiteboard to malfunction. Follow these steps:

- **Update Zoom**:

    - Open Zoom, go to **Settings > Check for Updates**, and install the latest version.

- **Use a supported browser**:

    - Zoom Whiteboard works best on **Google Chrome, Microsoft Edge, or Safari**.

    - Clear browser cache to remove outdated data (**Settings > Clear Browsing Data**).

Troubleshooting Sync Problems

1. Checking Zoom Whiteboard Status

If your whiteboard isn't updating, check if there's an outage:

- Visit <u>Zoom Service Status</u> to see if Zoom's cloud services are experiencing issues.

- If Zoom is down, wait until the service is restored.

2. Refreshing the Whiteboard

Sometimes, a simple refresh can resolve sync issues:

- **Close and reopen** the Whiteboard.

- Click the **"Refresh" button** (if available) in your Whiteboard interface.

- If using a browser, press **Ctrl + F5 (Windows) or Command + Shift + R (Mac)** to force a refresh.

3. Resolving Delayed Updates

If changes aren't appearing for all participants:

- Ensure everyone has a **stable internet connection** (refer to previous troubleshooting steps).

- **Check user permissions**:

  - Go to **Whiteboard settings** and ensure users have "Editor" access, not just "Viewer."

- **Manually save progress**:

  - Click **Save/Export** in Whiteboard to create a backup before refreshing.

- **Ask all participants to reload the Whiteboard**:

  - This forces their session to reconnect to Zoom's cloud storage.

4. Recovering Missing Content

If elements disappear unexpectedly:

- **Check Whiteboard version history**:

  - Zoom Whiteboard **automatically saves versions**. Navigate to **File > Version History** to restore an earlier version.

- **Undo accidental deletions**:

  - Press **Ctrl + Z (Windows) or Command + Z (Mac)** to undo recent actions.

- **Verify sync status**:

  - If using multiple devices, check if content appears on another device.

5. Fixing Conflicting Whiteboard Versions

If multiple copies of the same whiteboard exist:

- **Check timestamps**:

  - Open each version and compare modification times.

- **Merge content manually**:

  o Copy elements from different versions into a new, unified Whiteboard.

- **Set a primary whiteboard**:

  o Assign one document as the official version and delete unnecessary duplicates.

Preventing Future Connectivity and Sync Issues

1. Best Practices for a Stable Connection

- **Use a reliable ISP**: Choose an internet provider with strong uptime and customer support.

- **Set up a backup network**: Have a mobile hotspot or secondary Wi-Fi as an alternative.

- **Enable automatic Zoom updates**: Keep your software current to avoid compatibility issues.

2. Improving Sync Reliability

- **Save frequently**: Although Zoom auto-saves, manually saving ensures data is preserved.

- **Limit excessive elements**: Too many images, videos, or layers may slow down syncing.

- **Coordinate editing**: Have one person edit at a time to avoid conflicting changes.

3. Reporting Persistent Issues to Zoom Support

If problems continue, reach out to Zoom Support:

- **Submit a support ticket** at Zoom Support.

- **Provide error messages or screenshots** to help diagnose the issue.

- **Join Zoom user forums** to see if others have experienced similar issues.

Final Thoughts

Connectivity and sync problems can be frustrating, but with the right troubleshooting steps, most issues can be resolved quickly. By maintaining a stable internet connection, keeping Zoom updated, and following best practices, users can enjoy a seamless experience with Zoom Whiteboard.

If you continue to face persistent issues, consider reaching out to **Zoom's technical support** or consulting with your **organization's IT department**. The next section will explore **security and privacy considerations**, ensuring that your Whiteboard content remains protected while collaborating online.

6.1.2 File and Data Loss Recovery

Losing files or data while working on **Zoom Whiteboard** can be frustrating, especially when collaborating on important projects. Fortunately, Zoom provides several ways to recover lost content, whether due to accidental deletion, connectivity issues, or system crashes. In this section, we will explore the possible causes of data loss, recovery methods, and best practices to prevent future issues.

Understanding the Causes of Data Loss

Before diving into recovery solutions, it is essential to understand **why file or data loss happens** in Zoom Whiteboard. Some of the most common reasons include:

1. **Accidental Deletion** – A user may mistakenly delete a whiteboard or an important element while editing.

2. **Session Expiration** – If a whiteboard was created in a temporary session (such as a meeting) and not saved, it may not be available later.

3. **Syncing Errors** – Poor internet connectivity or a failure to sync with Zoom's cloud storage may result in missing updates.

4. **Software Glitches or Crashes** – Unexpected errors in Zoom or the device being used can lead to data loss.

5. **Insufficient Permissions** – If a user does not have the right permissions, they may not be able to see or recover certain whiteboards.

6. **Cloud Storage Issues** – If Zoom's cloud service experiences downtime or an account loses access due to licensing issues, data may temporarily become unavailable.

Now that we have identified the main reasons for data loss, let's explore how to recover lost whiteboards and prevent future issues.

Recovering Deleted or Lost Whiteboards

Zoom provides multiple ways to recover lost whiteboards, depending on how the data was lost. The following steps cover different scenarios:

1. Recovering Whiteboards from the Zoom Whiteboard Dashboard

If a whiteboard has been accidentally deleted or lost, the first place to check is **Zoom Whiteboard's dashboard**. Follow these steps:

1. **Log in to Zoom** at zoom.us and navigate to **Whiteboard** in the left-hand menu.

2. **Look for the missing whiteboard** in the list. If it was recently edited, it should appear in **Recent Whiteboards**.

3. **Use the search bar** to find the whiteboard by name or keywords.

4. **Check the Trash or Archived Whiteboards** – If the whiteboard was deleted, it might still be recoverable. Zoom stores deleted whiteboards for a certain period before permanently removing them.

5. **Restore the whiteboard** if found in the Trash by clicking **Restore**.

2. Using Version History to Restore Changes

If you lost part of your whiteboard but not the entire file, Zoom allows you to view and restore previous versions:

1. Open the whiteboard in **Edit Mode**.

2. Click on the **Version History** option (if available).

3. Browse through previous versions to find the correct one.

4. Click **Restore** to revert to the selected version.

3. Recovering Whiteboards from Cloud Storage (For Zoom Business Users)

For organizations using **Zoom Business, Enterprise, or Education plans**, whiteboards may be stored in **Zoom Cloud Storage**. If a whiteboard is missing:

1. Log in to **Zoom Admin Console**.

2. Navigate to **Whiteboard Management** under **Admin Settings**.

3. Look for backups or saved versions of whiteboards.

4. Restore the desired file.

4. Checking Local Device Cache for Unsaved Work

If Zoom crashed before saving your work, some data might still be stored locally:

- On **Windows**: Check C:\Users\[YourUsername]\AppData\Local\Zoom\Temp.

- On **Mac**: Go to ~/Library/Application Support/Zoom/Temp.

- On **Mobile Devices**: If working from a phone or tablet, check for auto-saved files in the Zoom app.

If files are found, they may need to be manually imported back into Zoom.

5. Contacting Zoom Support for Assistance

If none of the above methods work, you may need help from Zoom's support team:

- **Submit a support ticket** via Zoom Support.

- Provide details such as:

  o The whiteboard's name (if known).

  o The approximate date/time it was last edited.

  o Any actions that led to the data loss.

Zoom's team may be able to retrieve your whiteboard if it is still stored on their servers.

Preventing Future Data Loss

While recovery methods exist, **preventing data loss** is the best approach. Here are some essential tips:

1. Enable Auto-Save Features

- Always save whiteboards manually before closing a session.

- Use Zoom's auto-save or cloud backup features when available.

- If collaborating in a meeting, designate a team member to ensure that important work is saved before ending the session.

2. Regularly Backup Important Whiteboards

- Export whiteboards as PDFs or images to maintain a backup outside of Zoom.

- Use third-party cloud storage (such as Google Drive, OneDrive, or Dropbox) to store backups of critical whiteboards.

- Take screenshots of crucial content during brainstorming sessions.

3. Improve Internet Stability to Prevent Sync Errors

- Use a wired connection or a stable Wi-Fi network to avoid losing data due to connectivity issues.

- If working remotely, consider using a backup internet connection (such as a mobile hotspot).

- Check for Zoom server status at status.zoom.us before working on important projects.

4. Manage User Permissions to Avoid Accidental Deletion

- Limit editing access to trusted team members.

- Use role-based permissions to prevent unauthorized users from deleting or modifying whiteboards.

- Educate team members on how to properly save and manage whiteboards.

5. Keep Zoom Software Updated

- Ensure that you and your team are using the latest version of Zoom.

- Enable automatic updates on your device to receive the latest security and stability improvements.

Final Thoughts

Losing important whiteboards can be a stressful experience, but Zoom Whiteboard offers multiple ways to recover lost data—whether through built-in recovery tools, version history, or cloud backups. By implementing best practices such as auto-saving, frequent backups, and proper user permissions, users can minimize the risk of data loss and ensure a smooth collaborative experience.

If you ever encounter an issue that cannot be resolved using the methods outlined in this section, contacting Zoom Support should be the next step. They may be able to recover lost files or provide further assistance.

With the right precautions in place, you can confidently use Zoom Whiteboard without worrying about losing valuable content.

6.1.3 Whiteboard Access and Permission Issues

One of the most common challenges users face when using Zoom Whiteboard is dealing with access and permission issues. Whether you are a host, co-host, participant, or guest user, understanding how permissions work and how to troubleshoot related issues can significantly enhance your experience.

This section will cover:

- How Zoom Whiteboard permissions work

- Common access issues and their causes

- Step-by-step troubleshooting solutions

- Best practices for managing permissions

Understanding Zoom Whiteboard Permissions

Zoom Whiteboard permissions determine who can view, edit, and manage a whiteboard. Permissions are primarily controlled by:

- The role of the user (host, co-host, participant, guest, etc.)

- The whiteboard's sharing settings (private, shared within an organization, public, etc.)

- Zoom account settings and restrictions (admin-defined policies, security settings, etc.)

Types of Zoom Whiteboard Access

There are several levels of access in Zoom Whiteboard:

1. **Owner** – The person who created the whiteboard. They have full control over sharing, editing, and deleting the whiteboard.

2. **Editors** – Users who can edit the whiteboard. They can draw, add elements, and make modifications but may not have full management rights.

3. **Viewers** – Users who can only view the whiteboard without making any modifications.

4. **Guests** – Users outside of your Zoom organization who are given access (may be restricted based on company policies).

Common Access Issues and Their Causes

1. "You do not have permission to access this whiteboard."

Possible Causes:

- The whiteboard owner has restricted access to certain users or groups.

- Your Zoom account does not have the required permissions to view shared whiteboards.

- The whiteboard is only available to users within a specific organization, and your account is external.

Solution:

- Check with the whiteboard owner to confirm that your email or Zoom account is listed under authorized users.

- If the whiteboard is restricted to an organization, log in using an account that belongs to the same domain.

- Ask the owner to change the sharing settings in Zoom Whiteboard to allow external users if necessary.

---

2. "You can view this whiteboard but cannot edit it."

Possible Causes:

- The whiteboard is set to **"View Only" mode** for certain users.
- The **owner has not granted edit permissions** to your account.
- You are accessing the whiteboard as a **guest without proper permissions**.

Solution:

- Ask the owner to **adjust your role** to "Editor" in the whiteboard settings.
- If you are a guest, request the owner to **enable editing for external users**.
- Ensure you are **logged in with the correct Zoom account** associated with the shared whiteboard.

---

3. "Whiteboard not found" or "Access revoked" message appears

Possible Causes:

- The **whiteboard has been deleted** by the owner.
- The owner has **revoked access** or removed you from the list of authorized users.
- There is a syncing issue between Zoom's cloud storage and your device.

Solution:

- Contact the owner and ask if the whiteboard was **deleted or moved** to another location.
- If the access was revoked by mistake, request the owner to **re-share the whiteboard**.
- Log out and log back into Zoom to refresh permissions and sync your access.

How to Troubleshoot Whiteboard Access Issues Step by Step

Step 1: Verify Your Account and Permissions

- Log into **Zoom Web Portal** and navigate to **Whiteboards**.

- Check if the whiteboard is listed under **"My Whiteboards"** or **"Shared with Me"**.

- If you cannot find it, confirm with the owner that you have been granted access.

Step 2: Adjust Whiteboard Sharing Settings

- If you are the owner, go to **Whiteboard Settings** and review:

  o Who can access the whiteboard? (Only me, specific users, anyone in the organization, etc.)

  o What permissions do they have? (Can view, can comment, can edit)

  o Is the whiteboard restricted to signed-in users only?

- If necessary, modify sharing settings to **include the correct users or enable guest access**.

Step 3: Check Zoom Admin Policies (For Business and Enterprise Users)

- If you are using a **corporate Zoom account**, some permissions might be restricted by **Zoom Admins**.

- Ask your IT department to check **admin policies** and ensure external collaboration is allowed.

Step 4: Refresh and Reauthenticate Your Zoom Session

- Log out and log back into **your Zoom account**.

- Clear browser cache and cookies if using Zoom Whiteboard via the web.

- Restart the **Zoom desktop app** to apply updated permissions.

Step 5: Use an Alternative Access Method

- If you cannot open the whiteboard within a **Zoom meeting**, try accessing it from the **Zoom Web Portal**.

- If using a mobile device, switch to a desktop or vice versa to check if the issue is device-specific.

Best Practices for Managing Zoom Whiteboard Permissions

1. Define Access Roles Clearly

- Assign **specific roles** (owner, editor, viewer) to prevent confusion.

- Use **organization-wide settings** to ensure standard access policies.

2. Regularly Review and Update Access Lists

- Remove **inactive users** from shared whiteboards to maintain security.

- Periodically **review permissions** to avoid unnecessary access restrictions.

3. Use Zoom Admin Controls for Enterprise Security

- If working in a corporate environment, configure **security policies** to **control guest access** and **data privacy settings**.

4. Educate Your Team on Permission Management

- Provide **training on Zoom Whiteboard access settings**.

- Encourage users to **follow best practices** to prevent access issues.

Final Thoughts

Understanding and troubleshooting whiteboard access and permission issues is crucial for smooth collaboration in Zoom Workplace. By properly managing permissions, proactively addressing issues, and following best practices, users can enhance their Zoom Whiteboard experience and ensure efficient teamwork.

If you continue to face access problems, consider reaching out to Zoom Support or referring to Zoom's official documentation for additional guidance.

6.2 Security and Privacy Considerations

6.2.1 Managing User Access and Permissions

As digital collaboration becomes more common, ensuring security and privacy in online tools like Zoom Whiteboard is critical. Whether you're using Zoom Whiteboard for business meetings, educational sessions, or creative brainstorming, properly managing user access and permissions helps protect your data and maintain control over shared content.

This section explores best practices for managing user roles, permissions, and security settings to ensure a safe and efficient collaboration environment.

Understanding User Roles in Zoom Whiteboard

Zoom provides different **user roles** to help manage who can **view, edit, and manage** whiteboards. These roles determine the level of access each participant has.

1. Admins (Zoom Account Owners and Admins)

- Have full control over whiteboard settings, permissions, and security configurations for the entire organization.

- Can enable or disable whiteboard access for specific users or groups.

- Can integrate Zoom Whiteboard with SSO (Single Sign-On), domain restrictions, and external authentication methods to enhance security.

- Can enforce policies like data retention and automatic deletion of old whiteboards.

2. Whiteboard Owners (Creators)

- The person who creates a whiteboard is automatically its owner.

- Can edit, delete, share, and change permissions for the whiteboard.

- Can invite others to collaborate and determine their level of access.

- Can restrict or grant access to specific Zoom meetings, teams, or external users.

3. Editors (Collaborators with Editing Access)

- Can add, modify, and delete content on a shared whiteboard.

- Can interact with shapes, sticky notes, text boxes, and media elements.

- Cannot change ownership or access permissions unless explicitly allowed.

4. Viewers (Read-Only Access)

- Can see the whiteboard but cannot make changes.

- Useful for sharing presentations, training materials, or finalized whiteboards with external stakeholders.

How to Manage User Access and Permissions

1. Setting Permissions for a Whiteboard

When creating or sharing a whiteboard, you can **customize access levels** based on user roles. Follow these steps to set permissions:

1. **Open Zoom Whiteboard** and go to the **whiteboard dashboard**.

2. Click on the whiteboard you want to share.

3. Select **"Share"** to open the sharing settings.

4. Choose who can access the whiteboard:

    o Specific individuals (via email invitation)

    o Members of your Zoom organization

    o Anyone with the link (optional, less secure)

5. Assign access levels:

    o Can edit (full collaborator access)

    o Can view (read-only mode)

6. Set expiration dates for shared access (optional).

7. Click **"Done"** to apply the settings.

2. Restricting Access to Certain Users or Teams

For sensitive whiteboards, you may want to restrict access to only specific teams or departments.

- Organization-wide restrictions: Limit whiteboard access to verified Zoom accounts within your company.

- Domain-based restrictions: Allow only users with an email from a specific domain (e.g., *@yourcompany.com*).

- Group permissions: Assign different whiteboard access levels based on team roles (e.g., Marketing, Engineering, HR).

3. Managing Permissions for External Users

If you need to collaborate with external users (clients, partners, or freelancers), consider the following:

✓ Use temporary access: Grant short-term editor or viewer access that expires after a project is completed.
✓ Enable guest restrictions: Prevent external users from downloading or exporting whiteboard content.
✓ Use password protection: Require a password for external users to access a shared whiteboard.
✓ Monitor guest activities: Regularly review and revoke access when external collaboration is no longer needed.

Enhancing Whiteboard Security

1. Enforcing Strong Authentication Methods

To prevent unauthorized access, Zoom Whiteboard supports various authentication methods:

- Single Sign-On (SSO): Securely log in using your company's identity provider (IDP).

- Multi-Factor Authentication (MFA): Require additional verification (e.g., SMS codes, authentication apps) before users can access whiteboards.

- OAuth and API Keys: Control integration with third-party apps and limit access to trusted software.

2. Protecting Against Data Leaks and Unauthorized Sharing

Security risks often arise from accidental **oversharing** or improper data management. Here's how to mitigate them:

- Disable public sharing: Prevent whiteboards from being accessible via open links.

- Restrict screenshot and export options: Control whether users can download, print, or export content.

- Audit access logs: Regularly review user activity to detect unauthorized access attempts.

- Enable watermarking: Add watermarks to sensitive whiteboards to track unauthorized sharing.

3. Automating Data Retention and Deletion Policies

To comply with data protection regulations, organizations should set automatic data retention rules:

- Auto-delete old whiteboards: Remove unused content after a specified period (e.g., 90 days).

- Backup and archive critical whiteboards: Save important whiteboards to secure cloud storage.

Monitoring and Managing Whiteboard Security in Large Organizations

For enterprises or educational institutions using Zoom Whiteboard at scale, security management requires **ongoing monitoring**:

1. Using Zoom Admin Dashboard for Security Oversight

Admins can access security reports via Zoom's Admin Dashboard to:

- Track whiteboard usage patterns
- Identify suspicious login attempts
- Review user access logs
- Manage inactive or orphaned whiteboards

2. Educating Users on Security Best Practices

Even the best security settings are ineffective if users are unaware of best practices. Organizations should:

- ✓ Train employees on whiteboard security policies
- ✓ Conduct regular audits to ensure compliance
- ✓ Provide security checklists for whiteboard creators

Final Thoughts: Building a Secure Whiteboarding Environment

Managing user access and permissions is essential for maintaining security and privacy in Zoom Whiteboard. By carefully configuring roles, authentication settings, and data policies, you can protect sensitive information while enabling seamless collaboration.

In the next section, we'll explore future trends in Zoom Whiteboard, including AI-powered automation and AR/VR integration, to see how digital collaboration is evolving.

6.2.2 Protecting Sensitive Data on Whiteboards

As organizations increasingly rely on digital collaboration tools, data security and privacy have become critical concerns. Zoom Whiteboard, like other cloud-based platforms, requires careful handling of sensitive information to prevent unauthorized access, data leaks, or compliance violations. This section explores the best practices, security settings, and risk mitigation strategies to protect sensitive data on Zoom Whiteboards effectively.

---

1. Understanding the Risks of Sharing Sensitive Data on Whiteboards

Before implementing security measures, it's important to recognize **potential risks** associated with using Zoom Whiteboard. Some common concerns include:

- Unauthorized Access: If whiteboards are shared carelessly, unauthorized users might view, edit, or delete important data.

- Data Leakage: Screenshots, copied content, or exported files may be distributed outside authorized teams.

- Weak Permissions: If access settings are too lenient, external users might gain control over confidential information.

- Accidental Deletion: Users with edit privileges might remove important data unintentionally.

- Compliance Risks: Organizations handling sensitive data (e.g., financial, medical, or legal information) must comply with regulations like GDPR, HIPAA, or SOC 2.

By understanding these risks, organizations can take proactive measures to ensure that sensitive data remains protected.

2. Best Practices for Securing Zoom Whiteboards

2.1 Controlling Access and Permissions

One of the most effective ways to protect data is by configuring whiteboard access permissions correctly. Zoom provides several levels of access, which should be carefully assigned based on user roles:

- Viewer – Can only view content but not make changes.

- Commenter – Can provide feedback without modifying the content.

- Editor – Can make changes to the whiteboard.

- Owner – Has full control over the whiteboard, including sharing settings.

Steps to Set Access Permissions Securely:

1. Use Organization-Only Access: Limit access to whiteboards only to users within your organization unless external sharing is necessary.

2. Enable Password Protection: If a whiteboard is shared externally, set a strong password to prevent unauthorized access.

3. Restrict Editing Privileges: Only allow trusted team members to modify whiteboard content, while others should have view/comment-only access.

4. Regularly Review and Update Access: Revoke permissions for former employees, contractors, or third parties who no longer need access.

5. Use Waiting Room and Authentication for Meetings: If sharing a whiteboard in a live session, enable Zoom's waiting room and user authentication to prevent unauthorized attendees from accessing it.

2.2 Implementing Data Encryption

Zoom applies end-to-end encryption (E2EE) to protect shared content, including whiteboards. However, users should also take extra precautions:

- Enable Encryption for Data at Rest and in Transit: Ensure that all whiteboard content is encrypted when stored and transferred.

- Use Secure Connections: Access Zoom Whiteboard only from trusted networks (avoid public Wi-Fi) and enable VPNs when necessary.

- Check Zoom's Security Features: Zoom regularly updates its security infrastructure, so always enable the latest encryption and security options available.

2.3 Managing File Sharing and Exporting

Whiteboards often contain valuable data, and exporting content poses security risks if not managed properly. To prevent data leaks, follow these guidelines:

1. Restrict File Exports: Disable or limit the ability to download, export, or copy content for unauthorized users.

2. Monitor File Transfers: If file sharing is necessary, use audit logs to track who exports whiteboard content.

3. Apply Watermarks to Exports: Adding watermarks to exported images or PDFs discourages unauthorized redistribution.

4. Use Zoom Cloud Storage Carefully: Store whiteboards in Zoom's cloud only when necessary, and ensure auto-deletion settings are in place for temporary files.

2.4 Using Multi-Factor Authentication (MFA) and Single Sign-On (SSO)

For an added layer of security, MFA and SSO should be enabled for all Zoom accounts that access whiteboards containing sensitive information:

- MFA (Multi-Factor Authentication): Requires users to verify their identity using an additional security code or biometric authentication.

- SSO (Single Sign-On): Allows users to log in using their organization's credentials, reducing the risk of compromised passwords.

How to Enable MFA for Zoom Whiteboard:

1. Navigate to Zoom Account Settings.

2. Select Security Settings.

3. Enable Two-Factor Authentication (2FA).

4. Choose an authentication method (e.g., Google Authenticator, SMS verification, email confirmation).

---

3. Ensuring Compliance with Data Protection Regulations

Many industries must follow strict data protection laws when handling sensitive information. Organizations using Zoom Whiteboard should ensure compliance with relevant regulations:

- GDPR (General Data Protection Regulation) – Protects personal data in the European Union (EU).

- HIPAA (Health Insurance Portability and Accountability Act) – Applies to healthcare data in the United States.

- SOC 2 (Service Organization Control 2) – Ensures secure data management practices for cloud-based services.

3.1 How to Make Zoom Whiteboard Compliant

1. Use Data Retention Policies: Automatically delete old whiteboards that contain personal or confidential data.

2. Enable Activity Logs: Track who accessed, edited, or shared a whiteboard.

3. Limit Third-Party Integrations: Be cautious when integrating Zoom Whiteboard with external apps (e.g., Google Drive, Dropbox) that might not comply with your organization's security policies.

4. Train Employees on Compliance: Conduct regular training to educate users on handling sensitive data securely.

4. Proactive Measures for Long-Term Security

Conduct Regular Security Audits

- Perform quarterly security audits to identify potential vulnerabilities in Zoom Whiteboard settings.

- Use penetration testing to check for security weaknesses.

Implement Incident Response Plans

- Establish clear protocols for data breaches, accidental sharing, and security threats.

- Maintain backup copies of critical whiteboards for recovery purposes.

Stay Updated with Zoom's Security Enhancements

- Follow Zoom's official security updates to enable newest security features.

- Join Zoom's user community to learn about best practices and emerging threats.

Conclusion

Protecting sensitive data on Zoom Whiteboard requires a combination of smart access controls, encryption, compliance measures, and user training. By implementing the best practices outlined in this chapter, organizations can enhance security, reduce risks, and ensure a safe digital collaboration environment.

By following strict access permissions, encryption protocols, compliance regulations, and security audits, businesses and individuals can leverage the power of Zoom Whiteboard without compromising sensitive information.

6.2.3 Compliance with Industry Standards

As organizations and individuals increasingly rely on digital collaboration tools, ensuring compliance with industry security and privacy standards is crucial. Zoom Whiteboard, like other digital whiteboarding tools, is subject to various regulatory requirements that govern data protection, access control, and overall cybersecurity. This section explores the key compliance frameworks, how Zoom Whiteboard aligns with them, and best practices for organizations to maintain regulatory adherence.

Understanding Compliance in Digital Collaboration

Compliance refers to the process of adhering to laws, regulations, and industry standards that dictate how digital platforms handle user data, security protocols, and access controls. Companies using Zoom Whiteboard must ensure their usage aligns with these requirements to protect sensitive information and mitigate potential risks.

Some common concerns regarding compliance in digital whiteboarding include:

- **Data Privacy:** How is user information stored, processed, and shared?

- **Access Control:** Who can view, edit, and download content on the whiteboard?

- **Data Retention and Deletion:** How long is whiteboard data stored, and how can it be permanently removed?

- **Encryption and Security Measures:** What steps are taken to prevent unauthorized access or data breaches?

To address these concerns, Zoom Whiteboard follows several **key industry standards** and provides built-in security features that organizations can leverage for compliance.

Key Compliance Standards for Zoom Whiteboard

1. General Data Protection Regulation (GDPR)

The General Data Protection Regulation (GDPR) is a European Union regulation that governs how organizations handle personal data of EU citizens. It applies to any company that processes data from individuals within the EU, even if the company itself is located outside Europe.

How Zoom Whiteboard Supports GDPR Compliance:

- User Consent and Data Transparency: Zoom Whiteboard allows organizations to control what data is collected and inform users about its usage.

- Right to Access and Erasure: Users can request access to their stored whiteboard data and delete it when necessary.

- Data Encryption: Information shared on Zoom Whiteboard is encrypted in transit and at rest to prevent unauthorized access.

2. Health Insurance Portability and Accountability Act (HIPAA)

The Health Insurance Portability and Accountability Act (HIPAA) is a U.S. regulation that protects sensitive patient information. Any organization using Zoom Whiteboard in the healthcare sector must ensure HIPAA compliance to safeguard patient confidentiality.

How Zoom Whiteboard Supports HIPAA Compliance:

- Secure Authentication: Multi-factor authentication (MFA) ensures that only authorized personnel can access patient-related whiteboards.

- Audit Trails: Organizations can track who accessed and modified a whiteboard, ensuring full transparency in medical discussions.

- Data Protection Measures: Encrypted storage and access logs prevent unauthorized data exposure.

Important Note: Zoom Whiteboard itself does not automatically ensure HIPAA compliance. Organizations must configure settings and sign a Business Associate Agreement (BAA) with Zoom to use it for HIPAA-regulated work.

3. ISO/IEC 27001: Information Security Management

ISO/IEC 27001 is an internationally recognized standard for managing information security risks. It helps organizations establish a framework for protecting sensitive data and ensuring business continuity.

How Zoom Whiteboard Aligns with ISO 27001:

- **Risk Management:** Zoom follows best practices for identifying and mitigating security risks.

- **Access Controls:** Organizations can enforce role-based permissions to limit whiteboard access.

- **Regular Security Audits:** Zoom undergoes independent audits to verify its security posture.

4. Family Educational Rights and Privacy Act (FERPA)

FERPA is a U.S. law that protects the privacy of student education records. Schools and universities using Zoom Whiteboard must ensure that student information is not improperly shared.

How Zoom Whiteboard Supports FERPA Compliance:

- **Student Data Protection:** Only authorized educators and students can access class whiteboards.

- **Privacy Controls:** Educators can restrict the ability to download or share content.

- **Data Retention Policies:** Schools can control how long student data is stored before deletion.

5. California Consumer Privacy Act (CCPA)

The **CCPA** is a California law that grants consumers greater control over their personal data. It requires businesses to disclose what information they collect and give users the right to opt out.

How Zoom Whiteboard Supports CCPA Compliance:

- **User Data Control:** Users can request to view, edit, or delete their whiteboard data.

- **Opt-Out Mechanism:** Organizations can configure settings to limit data tracking.

- **Data Security Measures:** Encryption and restricted access protect consumer data from breaches.

Best Practices for Ensuring Compliance in Zoom Whiteboard

While Zoom Whiteboard provides built-in security features to support compliance, organizations must also take proactive steps to protect their data.

1. Implement Role-Based Access Control (RBAC)

- Assign specific roles (e.g., viewer, editor, admin) to ensure only authorized users can modify sensitive whiteboards.

- Restrict external sharing of confidential data.

2. Enable Multi-Factor Authentication (MFA)

- Require users to verify their identity before accessing Zoom Whiteboard.

- This prevents unauthorized access even if login credentials are compromised.

3. Set Up Data Retention Policies

- Define how long whiteboard data should be stored.

- Regularly delete unnecessary or outdated whiteboards to minimize risk exposure.

4. Use Encrypted Storage and Secure Backups

- Ensure all whiteboard content is encrypted at rest and in transit.

- Store backups in a secure location to prevent accidental loss of important data.

5. Regularly Audit and Monitor Whiteboard Activity

- Enable logging to track who accessed and modified whiteboards.

- Conduct periodic compliance audits to ensure adherence to security policies.

6. Educate Users on Data Protection Best Practices

- Train employees, educators, or students on securely using Zoom Whiteboard.

- Encourage responsible sharing and data handling practices.

Future Compliance Trends for Digital Collaboration Tools

As digital collaboration continues to evolve, compliance standards will also become more sophisticated. Some emerging trends include:

1. AI-Driven Compliance Monitoring

- Automated systems will help organizations detect and prevent data breaches.
- AI tools will analyze user behavior to flag potential security risks.

2. Stronger Global Data Privacy Laws

- Countries worldwide are introducing stricter data protection laws.
- Organizations will need to adapt to comply with multiple international regulations.

3. Enhanced User Control over Personal Data

- Future updates to Zoom Whiteboard may offer more granular privacy settings.
- Users will have greater transparency on how their data is stored and shared.

Conclusion

Compliance with industry security standards is a critical aspect of using Zoom Whiteboard safely and effectively. By aligning with frameworks such as GDPR, HIPAA, ISO 27001, FERPA, and CCPA, Zoom Whiteboard helps organizations maintain data security and privacy. However, compliance is not automatic—organizations must configure security settings, enforce best practices, and stay updated with evolving regulations.

By implementing strong security measures, conducting regular audits, and educating users, organizations can leverage Zoom Whiteboard for productive collaboration while ensuring full compliance with legal and industry requirements.

6.3 The Future of Zoom Whiteboard and Digital Collaboration

6.3.1 AI and Automation in Whiteboarding

Introduction

As digital collaboration tools continue to evolve, artificial intelligence (AI) and automation are reshaping the way teams interact and create content. Zoom Whiteboard, a key component of Zoom Workplace, is no exception. AI-driven features are expected to make whiteboarding more intuitive, efficient, and productive, enabling users to focus more on ideation and strategic thinking rather than the mechanics of using the tool.

This section explores how AI and automation are transforming Zoom Whiteboard, from smart content generation and automated organization to intelligent suggestions and enhanced accessibility.

1. Smart Content Generation and Recognition

One of the most exciting advancements in AI-driven whiteboarding is the ability to generate and recognize content automatically. Zoom Whiteboard is expected to incorporate AI-powered tools that assist users in creating structured and visually appealing boards with minimal effort.

Handwriting and Shape Recognition

AI-powered handwriting recognition enables users to write notes or draw diagrams by hand, which are then converted into readable text or precise shapes. This feature enhances the clarity of whiteboard content, making it easier for teams to collaborate effectively.

Example use cases:

- A team brainstorming ideas can quickly jot down concepts, and AI will neatly format them into legible text.

- A designer sketching wireframes can rely on AI to transform rough sketches into refined shapes.

Auto-Diagramming and Flowchart Creation

AI can assist in creating structured diagrams by automatically recognizing relationships between elements. If a user starts drawing arrows between concepts, the AI can suggest or complete flowcharts, decision trees, or process diagrams.

Example use cases:

- Project managers can sketch a basic workflow, and AI will refine it into a professional-looking process map.

- Educators can create mind maps in real time, with AI automatically categorizing and linking topics.

Predictive Text and Idea Expansion

AI-driven whiteboards may also feature predictive text and idea expansion, helping users brainstorm by suggesting relevant terms, concepts, or follow-up questions based on the discussion.

Example use cases:

- AI suggests additional discussion points based on meeting context.

- Teams can use AI-generated prompts to explore new angles of a topic.

---

2. Automated Organization and Smart Formatting

As whiteboards grow in complexity, AI can help organize and format content automatically, ensuring clarity and readability.

Auto-Align and Layout Optimization

AI-driven auto-align features can rearrange elements on a whiteboard for better visual balance. This eliminates the need for manual adjustments and ensures that all content remains structured.

Example use cases:

- A messy brainstorming board is automatically cleaned up, aligning sticky notes and text boxes into an easy-to-read format.

- A complex wireframe is optimized for better spacing and symmetry.

Smart Categorization and Tagging

AI can analyze the content on a whiteboard and suggest categories, labels, or tags, making it easier to navigate and retrieve information.

Example use cases:

- AI detects recurring themes in a brainstorming session and groups similar ideas together.

- Project whiteboards are automatically tagged based on content keywords, simplifying searchability.

Content Summarization and Meeting Recaps

AI-powered summarization tools can analyze whiteboard content and generate concise summaries, which can be shared with participants after meetings.

Example use cases:

- After a strategy session, AI provides a bullet-point summary of key takeaways.

- Teams receive an AI-generated action plan based on meeting discussions.

3. Intelligent Collaboration and Real-Time Assistance

AI can enhance real-time collaboration by providing instant suggestions, insights, and workflow optimizations.

Smart Recommendations for Participants

Based on whiteboard content, AI can recommend relevant contributors who may have expertise in a given topic.

Example use cases:

- AI suggests inviting a marketing expert to a whiteboard discussion on branding strategies.

- AI notifies project managers when their input is required for a workflow discussion.

AI-Powered Voice Commands and Assistants

Future iterations of Zoom Whiteboard may integrate voice recognition, allowing users to interact with the board using natural language commands.

Example use cases:

- A user says, "Create a new brainstorming board," and AI sets up a structured layout automatically.

- A presenter asks, "Summarize key points from this session," and AI generates a concise overview.

Automated Task Assignment and Workflow Integration

AI can analyze whiteboard discussions and automatically convert key points into actionable tasks, assigning them to relevant team members.

Example use cases:

- AI detects action items from a meeting and syncs them with project management tools.

- AI-generated to-do lists help teams stay organized without manual input.

4. Enhancing Accessibility and Inclusion

AI and automation can make Zoom Whiteboard more accessible to a diverse range of users, including those with disabilities or language barriers.

Real-Time Language Translation

AI-driven language translation can enable global teams to collaborate seamlessly by providing instant translations of whiteboard content.

Example use cases:

- An international team collaborates without language barriers, with AI translating discussions in real time.

- Multilingual whiteboards enable smooth cross-border collaboration.

Voice-to-Text and Text-to-Speech Features

AI-powered transcription services can convert spoken words into written text, ensuring that discussions are captured accurately.

Example use cases:

- AI converts meeting discussions into whiteboard notes automatically.

- Visually impaired users can use text-to-speech tools to engage with whiteboard content.

Adaptive UI and Personalization

AI can personalize the whiteboarding experience based on user preferences, improving usability for individuals with different working styles.

Example use cases:

- Users with visual impairments can enable high-contrast mode and voice guidance.

- AI suggests interface adjustments based on usage patterns.

5. Challenges and Considerations of AI in Whiteboarding

While AI and automation offer significant advantages, there are challenges to consider.

Data Privacy and Security Risks

AI-powered features rely on data collection and analysis, raising concerns about security and privacy. Organizations must ensure compliance with data protection regulations.

Balancing AI Automation with Human Creativity

While AI can assist in structuring and organizing content, it should not replace human creativity. Maintaining a balance between automation and user-driven input is crucial.

Learning Curve and Adoption Barriers

Integrating AI into whiteboarding may require users to adapt to new workflows. Proper training and user-friendly implementations are key to successful adoption.

Conclusion

AI and automation are revolutionizing the way teams collaborate using Zoom Whiteboard. From smart content generation and predictive suggestions to real-time language translation and automated task management, these innovations are set to enhance productivity and creativity. While challenges such as data security and adoption barriers exist, the future of AI-powered whiteboarding is promising, paving the way for more intuitive and efficient digital collaboration.

As Zoom continues to evolve, embracing these AI-driven features will empower teams to work smarter, faster, and more effectively than ever before.

6.3.2 Enhancing AR/VR Integration

The future of digital collaboration is evolving rapidly, and Augmented Reality (AR) and Virtual Reality (VR) are at the forefront of this transformation. As businesses, educators, and creative professionals seek more immersive ways to collaborate remotely, integrating AR/VR with Zoom Whiteboard has the potential to revolutionize how we brainstorm, plan, and communicate visually.

In this section, we will explore:

- The current state of AR/VR in digital collaboration

- How AR/VR can enhance the Zoom Whiteboard experience

- Potential use cases across different industries

- Challenges and considerations in implementing AR/VR

- Future trends and developments

---

1. The Current State of AR/VR in Digital Collaboration

Augmented Reality (AR) and Virtual Reality (VR) have already made significant strides in industries like gaming, healthcare, and architecture. However, their adoption in workplace collaboration and digital whiteboarding is still in its early stages.

Currently, many organizations use VR meeting spaces (e.g., Meta Horizon Workrooms, Spatial, and Microsoft Mesh) to create virtual environments for remote teamwork. These platforms allow users to interact with digital objects, simulate real-world workspaces, and engage with colleagues more naturally than traditional video conferencing.

Zoom has already introduced Zoom Immersive View, which creates a more engaging meeting experience by placing participants in a shared virtual background. The next logical step is to integrate AR/VR functionalities into Zoom Whiteboard, transforming it from a two-dimensional tool into a fully interactive, spatial workspace.

---

2. How AR/VR Can Enhance the Zoom Whiteboard Experience

Integrating AR/VR into Zoom Whiteboard would provide several key benefits:

2.1 3D Whiteboarding and Spatial Collaboration

Traditional digital whiteboards operate in a two-dimensional space, limiting the depth of interaction. With VR integration, users could work on a three-dimensional whiteboard, allowing them to:

- Manipulate 3D models and objects in real-time

- View designs from different angles, rotate objects, and scale elements dynamically

- Walk around their digital whiteboard in a virtual room, enabling a more natural collaborative environment

This is particularly valuable for engineering, architecture, and product design teams, who frequently work with 3D models.

2.2 Gesture and Voice Control for Hands-Free Interaction

AR/VR integration could introduce gesture-based controls, enabling users to:

- Draw and write with hand movements instead of using a mouse

- Move elements by simply grabbing and repositioning them in the air

- Use voice commands to activate tools, switch between whiteboards, or highlight key ideas

This hands-free approach would be especially beneficial for presenters, teachers, and facilitators who need to maintain engagement without constantly adjusting settings manually.

2.3 Enhanced Remote Collaboration and Presence

One of the biggest challenges in remote work is the lack of physical presence. With VR-enabled whiteboards, users can:

- See avatars of their colleagues in real time, creating a more immersive experience

- Use spatial audio to naturally hear voices coming from specific directions, simulating an in-person brainstorming session

- Collaborate more effectively by using virtual sticky notes, 3D sketches, and interactive mind maps

This could bridge the gap between in-person and virtual collaboration, making remote meetings more engaging and productive.

3. Potential Use Cases of AR/VR-Enabled Zoom Whiteboard

3.1 Business Meetings and Strategic Planning

Executives and teams can use VR whiteboards to:

- Conduct immersive brainstorming sessions

- Create and manipulate dynamic business models

- Visually map out complex strategic roadmaps

3.2 Education and Training

Teachers and corporate trainers can benefit from:

- Interactive learning environments, where students engage with virtual objects

- VR-based workshops, allowing for hands-on experience in a safe, controlled virtual space

- Immersive case studies, where students step into real-world simulations

3.3 Product Development and Engineering

For design teams, AR/VR-enhanced whiteboards could facilitate:

- Prototyping in 3D, where designers can manipulate models before manufacturing

- Simulating real-world physics, helping engineers test concepts virtually

- Collaborative design reviews, reducing the need for physical prototypes

3.4 Healthcare and Medical Collaboration

Doctors, surgeons, and medical professionals could:

- Annotate 3D medical scans and discuss diagnoses in virtual meetings

- Conduct remote training and surgical simulations using AR/VR-enhanced visuals

- Improve telemedicine consultations with interactive patient charts

4. Challenges and Considerations in Implementing AR/VR with Zoom Whiteboard

While the benefits of AR/VR integration are clear, several challenges must be addressed:

Hardware and Accessibility

- Not all users have access to high-quality VR headsets (e.g., Meta Quest, HTC Vive, Microsoft HoloLens)

- Organizations must invest in compatible hardware to make VR collaboration effective

Learning Curve and Adoption

- VR interfaces require training for new users

- Businesses may face resistance from employees unfamiliar with VR technology

Performance and Connectivity Issues

- AR/VR applications demand high-speed internet and powerful computing resources

- Performance issues could arise in regions with limited connectivity

Privacy and Security Concerns

- Companies must secure virtual workspaces to prevent unauthorized access

- Data encryption will be necessary to protect sensitive whiteboard content

5. The Future of AR/VR in Zoom Whiteboard

Despite these challenges, the potential of AR/VR-enhanced digital collaboration is immense. As technology advances, we can expect:

AI-Powered VR Assistance

- Virtual assistants that help users organize and optimize whiteboards

- AI-generated insights based on real-time discussions

Integration with the Metaverse

- Zoom Whiteboard could become part of a larger virtual office environment

- Teams could move seamlessly between Zoom Meetings and VR workspaces

More Affordable and Accessible VR Solutions

- Companies like Apple, Meta, and Microsoft are investing in lightweight, affordable AR/VR headsets

- As costs decrease, AR/VR whiteboarding could become a standard tool for remote collaboration

Conclusion

The integration of AR/VR into Zoom Whiteboard represents the next frontier in digital collaboration. By enabling 3D interaction, gesture control, and immersive brainstorming, these technologies can bridge the gap between remote and in-person teamwork.

While there are challenges to overcome, the future is promising. As hardware becomes more accessible, AI enhances usability, and Zoom continues to innovate, AR/VR-powered whiteboards may soon become a core tool for businesses, educators, and creatives alike.

Now is the time for organizations to start exploring and experimenting with AR/VR collaboration tools, preparing for a future where virtual and physical workspaces seamlessly merge.

6.3.3 The Next Generation of Virtual Collaboration

Introduction

The evolution of virtual collaboration has been transformative, particularly in the wake of the digital revolution and the shift toward remote and hybrid work environments. Tools like Zoom Whiteboard have already redefined the way teams communicate, brainstorm, and share ideas in real time. However, the future of virtual collaboration extends beyond our current capabilities. Emerging technologies, evolving work dynamics, and changing user expectations will shape the next generation of digital collaboration.

In this section, we will explore the future trajectory of virtual collaboration, focusing on technological advancements, user experience improvements, and potential industry disruptions that will influence how Zoom Whiteboard and similar tools evolve.

1. The Rise of AI-Driven Collaboration

AI-Powered Whiteboarding Assistance

Artificial intelligence (AI) is expected to play a pivotal role in the next generation of Zoom Whiteboard and digital collaboration tools. AI-powered whiteboarding will allow users to:

- **Auto-Generate Content** – AI will be able to recognize handwritten notes and convert them into structured text, generate flowcharts from rough sketches, and suggest templates based on meeting objectives.

- **Smart Organization** – AI can categorize and structure brainstorming sessions, automatically grouping related ideas and summarizing discussions into key points.

- **Real-Time Translation & Transcription** – AI-driven **speech-to-text** and **language translation** features will allow global teams to collaborate seamlessly, breaking down language barriers.

AI-Enhanced Productivity Features

- **Predictive Suggestions** – AI could suggest relevant past whiteboards, meeting notes, or templates based on the topic being discussed.

- **Automated Follow-Ups** – After a whiteboarding session, AI can generate summaries, highlight action items, and assign tasks to relevant team members.

- **Voice and Gesture Control** – Users may be able to interact with Zoom Whiteboard through voice commands or hand gestures, reducing the need for manual input.

2. Immersive Collaboration: AR and VR Integration

Virtual Reality (VR) Workspaces

One of the most anticipated innovations in virtual collaboration is the integration of Virtual Reality (VR) into platforms like Zoom Whiteboard. VR will enable users to:

- Step into a 3D Whiteboard Space – Instead of working on a flat, 2D canvas, users can interact with whiteboards in a fully immersive 3D environment.

- Manipulate Objects Naturally – Using VR controllers, users can grab, rotate, and move sticky notes, diagrams, or text boxes in a virtual space.

- Enhance Remote Presence – VR will simulate the feeling of being in a physical meeting room, making remote collaboration feel more engaging and personal.

Augmented Reality (AR) Enhancements

AR will bring interactive digital elements into the real world, allowing for:

- Holographic Whiteboards – Imagine being able to project a Zoom Whiteboard into a physical room, allowing hybrid teams to collaborate with both in-person and remote participants.

- Real-Time Object Recognition – AR could recognize real-world sketches, sticky notes, or physical whiteboards and instantly convert them into digital elements on Zoom Whiteboard.

- Smart Annotations – AR will enable users to overlay contextual information, such as previous notes, references, or real-time insights, onto the whiteboard without cluttering the workspace.

3. The Evolution of Cloud-Based and Cross-Platform Collaboration

Enhanced Cloud Capabilities

Cloud technology will continue to advance, providing:

- Seamless Cross-Device Collaboration – Users will be able to start a whiteboard session on their desktop, continue it on a tablet, and finalize it on their mobile device, without losing any content or formatting.

- Offline Mode with Smart Syncing – Future versions of Zoom Whiteboard will likely offer offline editing, where changes made without internet access will automatically sync once the user reconnects.

- AI-Driven Cloud Search – Intelligent search functions will allow users to find relevant past whiteboards, notes, or project plans based on keywords, topics, or even visual elements.

Integration with the Expanding Digital Workplace

As organizations increasingly adopt a digital-first approach, Zoom Whiteboard will need to seamlessly integrate with a broader range of workplace tools, including:

- Project Management Platforms (e.g., Trello, Asana, Jira) – Users can automatically link whiteboard elements to project tasks and track progress.

- CRM and Business Analytics Tools (e.g., Salesforce, Power BI) – Whiteboards used in sales or strategy meetings could pull real-time data from CRM platforms.

- Automation Platforms (e.g., Zapier, Microsoft Power Automate) – Users could create automated workflows where whiteboard notes trigger emails, task assignments, or document generation.

4. The Future of Hybrid and Remote Work Collaboration

Personalized and Adaptive Workspaces

The next generation of digital collaboration will focus on providing users with highly customizable and adaptive work environments, including:

- Personalized Whiteboard Dashboards – Users will be able to save their preferred templates, tools, and layouts, creating a custom workspace that adapts to their workflow.

- Context-Aware Smart Recommendations – Zoom Whiteboard might suggest specific brainstorming templates, meeting agendas, or relevant past discussions based on the current session's context.

- Dynamic User Roles and Permissions – Future whiteboarding platforms may automatically adjust user permissions based on meeting type, ensuring the right people have the right level of access.

Strengthening Engagement in Hybrid Meetings

With hybrid work models becoming the norm, Zoom Whiteboard will need to bridge the gap between in-office and remote participants through:

- Intelligent Meeting Assistants – AI-powered bots could summarize discussions, highlight key takeaways, and recommend relevant action items.

- Real-Time Polling and Engagement Tools – More interactive elements, like live polls, quizzes, and brainstorming games, will be integrated into the whiteboard experience.

- Seamless Multi-Device Interaction – Participants in a hybrid meeting will be able to interact with the same whiteboard from different devices, whether it's a laptop, tablet, smartboard, or AR headset.

5. Ethical Considerations and Security Innovations

As virtual collaboration evolves, ethical concerns and security risks must be addressed. The future of Zoom Whiteboard and similar platforms will likely focus on:

- Advanced Encryption and Compliance Standards – More robust data security measures will be implemented to protect sensitive corporate and educational information.

- Ethical AI and Data Privacy – AI-powered features must be designed to prioritize user privacy and transparency in data collection and analysis.

- Combatting Digital Fatigue – Future collaboration tools may incorporate AI-driven wellness features, such as suggesting breaks, improving interface design, or minimizing cognitive overload during prolonged sessions.

Conclusion

The next generation of virtual collaboration will go beyond simple video calls and shared documents—it will redefine how we work, interact, and co-create in digital environments.

Zoom Whiteboard is poised to evolve alongside AI, AR/VR, cloud computing, and workplace automation, making it a smarter, more interactive, and deeply integrated tool for teams worldwide. As these technologies develop, users will experience new ways of brainstorming, problem-solving, and decision-making, leading to a more efficient, engaging, and inclusive digital workplace.

By staying informed and adopting emerging trends, individuals and organizations can unlock the full potential of Zoom Whiteboard and stay ahead in the future of collaboration.

CHAPTER VII
Conclusion and Next Steps

7.1 Key Takeaways from This Guide

7.1.1 Recap of Essential Features

Throughout this guide, we have explored the many features of **Zoom Whiteboard**, learning how it can be used to enhance collaboration, creativity, and productivity. As we reach the conclusion of this book, it is helpful to reflect on the essential features we've covered and how they contribute to effective digital whiteboarding.

1. Accessing and Navigating Zoom Whiteboard

One of the first steps to mastering Zoom Whiteboard is understanding how to access and navigate it. Whether using the Zoom Web Portal, launching it within a Zoom Meeting, or accessing it on mobile devices, the flexibility of Zoom Whiteboard makes it an essential tool for both remote and hybrid work environments.

Navigating the whiteboard interface efficiently allows users to interact with various tools and features, including:

- The toolbar, which provides easy access to drawing, text, and media tools.

- The canvas, where users can create, organize, and expand their visual ideas.

- The layer and object management system, which helps structure complex whiteboards without clutter.

By familiarizing yourself with these elements, you can move seamlessly through Zoom Whiteboard and maximize its potential.

2. Creating and Managing Whiteboards

Creating a new whiteboard is a simple yet powerful action that can significantly impact your workflow. This guide has covered how to:

- Start a new whiteboard from scratch or using templates.

- Save and organize whiteboards effectively to ensure easy access.

- Share whiteboards with colleagues and team members for real-time collaboration.

A well-organized whiteboard allows for better communication and idea structuring, making it easier to reference and modify over time.

3. Essential Drawing and Annotation Tools

A whiteboard is only as effective as its tools, and Zoom Whiteboard provides a diverse set of annotation and drawing tools that enhance brainstorming and teamwork. Some of the most essential tools include:

- Pen, highlighter, and eraser tools, which allow for freehand sketching and note-taking.

- Shapes and lines, used for creating structured diagrams and process flows.

- Sticky notes and text boxes, which enable users to add written content without disrupting the visual flow of the whiteboard.

Mastering these tools allows you to visually communicate ideas in a way that is both clear and engaging.

4. Adding Media and Interactive Elements

Beyond basic drawing, Zoom Whiteboard supports the integration of various media elements, making it a dynamic and engaging platform. Users can:

- Insert images and PDFs to reference external content.

- Embed links and videos for additional resources.

- Use smart connectors to create logical relationships between ideas.

These features transform Zoom Whiteboard from a simple drawing tool into a multimedia collaboration hub, enabling more interactive and productive sessions.

5. Collaboration Features and Real-Time Editing

One of Zoom Whiteboard's standout features is its real-time collaboration capability. This book has highlighted the importance of:

- Inviting participants to contribute to the whiteboard.

- Commenting and feedback tools to streamline communication.

- Version history and recovery, which allows users to track changes and restore previous versions.

By leveraging these features, teams can work together efficiently, regardless of their physical location.

6. Advanced Techniques for Structuring Whiteboards

For users who want to elevate their whiteboarding experience, understanding how to structure and organize content is crucial. Some of the best techniques covered in this book include:

- Using layers to separate different elements for clarity.

- Grouping objects to keep related content together.

- Creating reusable templates to maintain consistency across projects.

These techniques are particularly valuable for teams working on complex projects, brainstorming sessions, or structured workflows.

7. Interactive Brainstorming and Mind Mapping

Zoom Whiteboard is an excellent tool for brainstorming and mind mapping, as it provides the flexibility needed for idea generation. This guide has explored methods such as:

- Setting up effective brainstorming sessions using visual tools.

- Using mind maps to expand ideas logically.

- Connecting ideas with flowcharts to create structured thought processes.

Teams that implement these techniques can boost creativity and streamline problem-solving.

8. Maximizing Productivity with Shortcuts and Integrations

Efficiency is key when using any digital tool, and Zoom Whiteboard offers several ways to improve productivity, including:

- Keyboard shortcuts and quick actions for faster navigation.

- Automation and AI-assisted features to simplify workflows.

- Integration with Zoom and third-party tools such as Google Drive and Microsoft 365.

These features help users save time and work smarter, making Zoom Whiteboard a valuable addition to any professional toolkit.

9. Real-World Applications and Use Cases

Throughout this book, we have explored various real-world applications of Zoom Whiteboard, including:

- Business meetings and strategy sessions, where teams can visualize concepts and plan projects.

- Education and remote learning, where instructors can engage students with interactive lessons.

- Creative and design work, where professionals can sketch, storyboard, and brainstorm new ideas.

By understanding how Zoom Whiteboard is used across different industries, users can tailor their approach to fit their specific needs.

10. Troubleshooting and Security Considerations

No tool is without challenges, and this guide has also provided solutions for common issues such as:

- Connectivity and sync problems, which can affect real-time collaboration.

- File and data loss recovery, ensuring that important whiteboards are never lost.

- Access and permission management, preventing unauthorized use of whiteboards.

Additionally, security and privacy considerations are essential for maintaining data integrity and confidentiality, making it important for users to:

- Manage user permissions effectively.

- Protect sensitive data with security settings.

- Ensure compliance with industry standards.

Final Thoughts

Mastering Zoom Whiteboard is not just about learning the technical aspects—it's about using the tool effectively to enhance communication, collaboration, and creativity. By understanding its essential features, applying best practices, and utilizing advanced techniques, users can fully unlock the potential of Zoom Whiteboard.

In the next sections of this conclusion, we will explore best practices for effective whiteboarding and discuss common mistakes to avoid to help you get the most out of this powerful collaboration tool.

7.1.2 Best Practices for Effective Whiteboarding

Zoom Whiteboard is a powerful tool for collaboration, brainstorming, and project planning. However, to maximize its potential, users should adopt best practices that enhance clarity, engagement, and efficiency. Whether you're using Zoom Whiteboard for business meetings, educational purposes, or creative design work, following structured guidelines will help you create more effective and impactful whiteboards.

This section outlines essential best practices for **effective whiteboarding**, covering preparation, organization, collaboration techniques, and productivity enhancements.

1. Preparing for a Productive Whiteboarding Session

Define Clear Objectives

Before starting a Zoom Whiteboard session, it is essential to define the **purpose** of the whiteboard. Ask yourself:

- What is the goal of this session? (Brainstorming, process mapping, project planning, etc.)
- Who will participate, and what are their roles?
- What outcomes do you expect by the end of the session?

A well-defined objective ensures that participants stay focused and that the whiteboard serves its intended purpose rather than becoming a cluttered, unstructured space.

Choose the Right Whiteboard Layout and Tools

Zoom Whiteboard offers different layouts, tools, and templates. Selecting the appropriate format can improve clarity and efficiency. Consider:

- Blank Whiteboards for freeform brainstorming.

- Templates for structured workflows like Kanban boards, SWOT analysis, or mind maps.

- Grids and Sections to organize content systematically.

Choosing the right setup before the session begins prevents unnecessary rearrangement later.

Set Up Access and Permissions in Advance

To avoid disruptions, configure participant access levels before the session starts. Zoom Whiteboard allows different permissions:

- View-only (for observers)

- Edit access (for active contributors)

- Facilitator mode (for moderators)

Granting the right level of control ensures a smooth experience and prevents accidental modifications or deletions.

2. Structuring and Organizing Your Whiteboard

Use Layers and Grouping for Better Organization

A whiteboard can become visually overwhelming if elements are scattered randomly. Use layers and grouping to maintain a structured format:

- Grouping related objects (e.g., clustering sticky notes by theme).

- Layering elements (placing text above images for clarity).

- Using shapes and colors to categorize information.

Maintain a Logical Flow

Ensure your whiteboard follows a clear left-to-right or top-to-bottom flow, making it easier for participants to follow. Common strategies include:

- Numbering sections for step-by-step processes.

- Using arrows and connectors to show relationships between ideas.

- Creating separate sections for brainstorming, decision-making, and action plans.

A structured layout prevents confusion and enhances readability.

Keep Text Concise and Legible

While whiteboards allow for freeform writing, maintaining readability is crucial:

- Use short bullet points instead of long paragraphs.

- Select clear, bold fonts for headings.

- Use contrasting colors for better visibility.

A well-organized whiteboard ensures that information is easy to absorb at a glance.

3. Enhancing Collaboration and Engagement

Encourage Active Participation

An effective whiteboard session requires engagement from all participants. Foster collaboration by:

- Assigning specific tasks (e.g., one person adds ideas, another organizes).

- Using sticky notes and voting tools to gather input.

- Encouraging participants to annotate directly instead of just observing.

Active involvement leads to richer discussions and better outcomes.

Use Real-Time Collaboration Features

Zoom Whiteboard includes real-time editing and commenting tools. Utilize these features to:

- Provide instant feedback on ideas.

- Track changes with version history.

- Use comment threads for discussion without cluttering the main board.

These tools ensure seamless collaboration, even in remote settings.

Establish Guidelines for Productive Sessions

To prevent disorganization, establish basic whiteboarding etiquette:

- Avoid overcrowding with too much content in one area.

- Use consistent colors and symbols for different types of information.

- Assign a facilitator to moderate and keep discussions on track.

Setting ground rules improves efficiency and keeps the session productive.

---

4. Leveraging Productivity Features

Save, Export, and Share Whiteboards Efficiently

To maximize the value of your whiteboards, use Zoom's export and sharing options:

- Save whiteboards as PDFs or images for easy reference.

- Share links with team members for asynchronous collaboration.

- Embed whiteboards into other tools like Slack, Trello, or project management apps.

Having a clear post-session strategy ensures that ideas are implemented rather than forgotten.

Integrate Zoom Whiteboard with Other Tools

For improved workflow, integrate Zoom Whiteboard with:

- Google Drive or OneDrive for cloud storage.

- Microsoft Teams or Slack for team communication.

- Project management tools (Asana, Jira, Trello) to track action items.

Using integrations helps streamline collaboration beyond the whiteboard session.

Automate and Optimize Whiteboard Processes

To save time, leverage automation and templates:

- Create pre-set templates for recurring meetings.

- Use AI-powered suggestions to auto-format content.

- Apply smart connectors to automatically link related elements.

Automating repetitive tasks allows for faster, more efficient whiteboarding sessions.

5. Avoiding Common Pitfalls in Whiteboarding

Preventing Clutter and Overcomplication

One of the biggest challenges in whiteboarding is avoiding clutter. Best practices include:

- Limiting text-heavy sections by using concise bullet points.

- Grouping related elements to reduce visual noise.

- Using color coding to differentiate between topics.

A clean, well-structured board enhances understanding and usability.

Managing Large Whiteboards Effectively

If a whiteboard contains extensive content, it can become difficult to navigate. Solutions include:

- Creating sections or pages for different topics.

- Using zoom and pan controls to navigate smoothly.

- Adding an index or navigation menu for easy reference.

These strategies help maintain control over complex whiteboards.

Ensuring Engagement in Virtual Sessions

Virtual whiteboarding sessions can sometimes become passive. Keep engagement high by:

- Using interactive exercises (brainstorming, ranking ideas).

- Encouraging voice and video input alongside whiteboard edits.

- Keeping sessions concise to prevent fatigue.

Interactive whiteboarding fosters higher participation and better outcomes.

Conclusion

By following these best practices, users can unlock the full potential of Zoom Whiteboard for collaboration, creativity, and productivity. Whether for business, education, or creative work, structuring content effectively, engaging participants, and utilizing advanced features will make your whiteboarding sessions more impactful and efficient.

The key takeaway? Zoom Whiteboard is more than just a digital canvas—it's a powerful tool for bringing ideas to life. Mastering these techniques will ensure you make the most out of every session.

7.1.3 Common Mistakes to Avoid

As with any digital tool, Zoom Whiteboard has a learning curve, and many users make common mistakes when getting started. Understanding these pitfalls can help you become more efficient, avoid frustration, and maximize your whiteboarding experience. In this section, we will explore the most frequent mistakes users make when using Zoom Whiteboard and provide actionable solutions to overcome them.

1. Not Utilizing All Available Tools

Many users limit themselves to only the basic tools, such as the pen and text box, while ignoring powerful features like sticky notes, shapes, connectors, and templates. This can lead to cluttered and inefficient whiteboards that do not fully leverage the platform's capabilities.

✅ **How to Avoid This Mistake:**

- Explore and experiment with each tool before starting a real collaboration session.
- Use **sticky notes** to structure ideas instead of relying solely on text.
- Leverage **smart connectors** for flowcharts and diagrams instead of drawing them manually.

- Try **pre-made templates** to save time and maintain a professional layout.

2. Failing to Organize the Whiteboard Properly

One of the biggest mistakes users make is **creating a messy, unstructured whiteboard** that becomes difficult to read and navigate. When multiple people collaborate on a single whiteboard, **lack of organization can lead to confusion** and inefficiency.

✅ **How to Avoid This Mistake:**

- Establish a **clear structure** before adding content—decide where different elements will be placed.

- Use **sections or frames** to separate ideas logically.

- Implement **consistent colors and shapes** to visually categorize different types of information.

- **Group related elements** together to maintain readability.

3. Not Setting Proper Access Permissions

Zoom Whiteboard offers multiple access levels (viewer, editor, owner), but **many users overlook these settings**, leading to security issues or collaboration roadblocks. Some users accidentally leave their whiteboards open to everyone, while others restrict access too much, preventing effective teamwork.

✅ **How to Avoid This Mistake:**

- Before sharing, **double-check access permissions** to ensure the right people can view or edit.

- Use **role-based access control** to limit unnecessary edits and maintain security.

- Regularly **review whiteboard access** and remove users who no longer need permissions.

4. Ignoring Collaboration Features

A common mistake is treating Zoom Whiteboard as **a solo tool** rather than a **real-time collaboration platform**. Some users do not take advantage of **commenting, reactions, and simultaneous editing**, which can improve teamwork and engagement.

✅ **How to Avoid This Mistake:**

- Use the **commenting feature** to give structured feedback instead of cluttering the board with extra text.

- Encourage **real-time collaboration** by inviting team members to edit and contribute.

- Utilize **reactions (e.g., thumbs up, checkmarks)** to streamline approval processes.

5. Forgetting to Save and Export Work Regularly

One of the biggest frustrations users face is losing work due to not saving or exporting their whiteboards. Although Zoom Whiteboard has an autosave function, some users forget to manually save versions or export their work for backup.

✅ **How to Avoid This Mistake:**

- Enable **autosave** and regularly **save manual versions** for important whiteboards.

- Use **export options (PDF, PNG, SVG)** to keep a copy outside Zoom.

- Periodically **download and back up** whiteboards to avoid accidental data loss.

6. Overcomplicating the Whiteboard

While Zoom Whiteboard offers a vast range of tools, **overusing too many elements** can lead to **visual clutter and confusion**. Some users add too many lines, colors, or overlapping text, making the board overwhelming.

✅ **How to Avoid This Mistake:**

- Keep it **simple and clear**—only include essential information.

- Use **a limited color palette** for easy readability.

- Avoid **overloading the board with excessive text**—use bullet points instead.

---

7. Not Taking Advantage of Keyboard Shortcuts

Many users do not know that Zoom Whiteboard **has keyboard shortcuts** that can speed up navigation and editing. Instead, they rely on manual selection, which slows down productivity.

✅ **How to Avoid This Mistake:**

- Learn essential shortcuts such as:
    - **Ctrl + Z** (Undo)
    - **Ctrl + Shift + Z** (Redo)
    - **Ctrl + C / Ctrl + V** (Copy/Paste)
    - **Ctrl + A** (Select all)
    - **Spacebar + Click & Drag** (Pan across the board)
- Print or keep a list of shortcuts nearby for quick reference.

---

8. Not Using Templates for Common Tasks

Instead of **recreating the same structures from scratch**, many users **miss out on the efficiency of templates**. This is a major time-wasting mistake, especially for teams that use **similar whiteboards frequently**.

✅ **How to Avoid This Mistake:**

- Browse **Zoom's template library** and use pre-built designs for common tasks.
- Create **custom templates** for your team's regular workflows.
- Save and **reuse templates** instead of designing from zero each time.

---

9. Ignoring Version History and Recovery Options

Accidental edits or deletions can cause panic, **especially when multiple users work on the same whiteboard**. Many people do not realize that Zoom Whiteboard **allows you to restore previous versions** to recover lost content.

✅ **How to Avoid This Mistake:**

- Use **version history** to track changes and revert to earlier versions if needed.

- Teach team members to **restore deleted elements** instead of redoing work.

10. Using Zoom Whiteboard in Isolation

Some users use Zoom Whiteboard **only within Zoom meetings**, instead of leveraging its potential **outside of meetings** for planning, brainstorming, and asynchronous collaboration.

✅ **How to Avoid This Mistake:**

- Use **Zoom Whiteboard as a standalone tool**—not just in meetings.

- Encourage team members to **collaborate on whiteboards before and after meetings**.

- Integrate **other Zoom tools (chat, breakout rooms, file sharing)** for a seamless workflow.

Final Thoughts

Avoiding these common mistakes will help you use Zoom Whiteboard more effectively, making your collaboration sessions smoother and more productive. By leveraging the right tools, maintaining organization, securing access, and optimizing teamwork, you can unlock the full potential of Zoom Whiteboard.

As you continue using this tool, stay curious and keep experimenting with new features. The more you practice and refine your approach, the better you'll become at creating engaging, structured, and visually compelling whiteboards.

Now that you have completed this guide, consider exploring advanced techniques and staying up to date with Zoom's latest features to enhance your digital collaboration experience.

Acknowledgment

Dear Reader,

*Thank you for choosing **"Zoom Whiteboard Made Simple: Unlock Your Creativity."** I sincerely appreciate your time and trust in this guide to help you navigate and master Zoom Whiteboard for collaboration, brainstorming, and productivity.*

In today's fast-paced digital world, effective collaboration is more important than ever. Whether you're using Zoom Whiteboard for business meetings, team projects, or personal organization, I hope this book has provided you with valuable insights, practical tips, and confidence to make the most of this powerful tool.

Writing this book was a journey of exploration and learning, and I am truly grateful to be able to share this knowledge with you. If this guide has helped simplify your experience, improve your workflow, or spark new ideas, then my goal has been fulfilled.

A special thank you to every reader, professional, student, and creative mind who is embracing new ways to collaborate and innovate. Your curiosity and willingness to learn inspire continuous growth in the world of digital collaboration.

If you found this book helpful, I would love to hear your thoughts! Your feedback and reviews help improve future editions and ensure that more readers can benefit from this knowledge.

Thank you once again for being part of this journey. Wishing you success, creativity, and seamless collaboration with Zoom Whiteboard!

Best regards,